CATHY'S CREEK

A Musical

Book by
ELISE FORIER

Music by
TINA LEAR

Lyrics by
TINA LEAR and ELISE FORIER

Dramatic Publishing
Woodstock, Illinois • England • Australia • New Zealand

This play is dedicated with great affection to
' Elena Terrone and Faye Moskowitz—
two women who have inspired us to listen to
the music of life and to face the toughest
times with faith and courage.

IMPORTANT BILLING AND CREDIT REQUIREMENTS

All producers of the Musical *must* give credit to the Author and Composer of the Musical in all programs distributed in connection with performances of the Musical and in all instances in which the title of the Musical appears for purposes of advertising, publicizing or otherwise exploiting the Musical and/or a production. The names of the author and Composer *must* also appear on a separate line, on which no other name appears, immediately following the title, and *must* appear in size of type not less than fifty percent (50%) the size of the title type. Biographical information on the Author and Composer, if included in the playbook, may be used in all programs. *In all programs this notice must appear:*

"Produced by special arrangement with
THE DRAMATIC PUBLISHING COMPANY of Woodstock, Illinois"

ACKNOWLEDGMENTS

Plays—and especially musicals—cannot be created without lots and lots of help. *Cathy's Creek* would not have been possible without the assistance of many people.

The authors would like to thank Stacie Burgua of the Whidbey Island Center for the Arts, who thought it would be a great idea if we wrote a new musical for the center's mainstage season and put us on the schedule, untried and unseen.

We are deeply grateful to Amy Windecker, who directed the play in its first incarnation, and the wonderful cast and crew at WICA, who faithfully hauled sod in and out of the theatre, changed the creek's water regularly, bandaged Tina's arm in the middle of the night and even flew up all the way from Texas to help us out.

Cathy's Creek would not be what it is today if not for the Waldo M. and Grace C. Bonderman Playwriting for Youth National Symposium, IUPUI, Indiana Repertory Theatre and the encouragement and help of the symposium's artistic director, Dr. Dorothy Webb. We are extremely grateful to the Bonderman's terrific artistic team: director Christopher Gurr, dramaturg Marge Betley and assistant Amy Ruth Goeldner McGraw, as well as the fantastic cast of actors and singers they assembled to help bring the play to its next level.

We are also very grateful to producer Steve Barberio and the actors and artists of Stages Theatre, who offered their talents, space and support to help us further shape and polish the script and score.

And, of course, we are also so grateful to Gayle Sergel, for tracking us down and giving us a chance to publish our work.

The music of *Cathy's Creek* would never have made it onto the page without the assistance of Dr. James Scott Balentine. He did lots of transcribing, taught Tina how to notate music and how to use the Finale software, and remains an indispensable mentor. Robbie Cribbs (faithful friend, recording engineer and tech support for Digital Performer issues), and the good people on the tech support end at MOTU and CodaMusic were also crucial to the birthing of this musical. Rob Hartmann was a font of good advice and excellent contacts. And thanks to Gabriel Shirley for convincing Tina to switch to a Mac.

There is also a long list of people who helped support us throughout this process by keeping us alive. They offered their homes, their working printers, they made us meals or took us out to dinner, they encouraged us to take our work into the world and they told us again and again that we were great and the show was going to be wonderful. These people are too numerous to count—they rank in the hundreds—and we are grateful to every single one of them, but we reserve special thanks to: George and Mary Lathrop, Ashley McConoughy, Tim Brod, Genevieve Forier, Mary Wells, Susan and John Anderson, Cousin Kaje, Ellen Dissanayake, Devra Kleiman, Ian Yeomans, Aimee Twargowski, Moya Olsen Lear, Wheezer, Germaine Stoll, Joni Mitchell, Chloe, Luke and Jesse Jackson, Courtney Campbell, Lynn Fuller, Donna Lee, Halim Dunsky, Amy Walker and her whole family, Walt Blackford, Shirley Jantz, Doug Shapiro, Melanie Holcomb and their daughters Amelia, Sophie and Ida Mae. THANK YOU for your kindness, courage and support. Especially, thank you for your love.

CATHY'S CREEK was originally commissioned and produced by the Whidbey Center for the Arts in Langley, Washington, in June 2001. It was directed by Amy Windecker, with set design by Amy and Bob Windecker, Beno Kennedy, Dave Gignac and Chris Spencer, costumes by Alex Martin and lighting by Ray Jarol. The stage managers were Dwight Zehm and Adriana Gallagher. The production's dramaturg was Vanessa DeWolfe. The music was played by Tina Lear and David Brogan.

Cathy	AMY WALKER
Jeanne	KARLA GILBERT
Myrna	MARY MCLEOD
Jack	TOM FISHER
Mike	LOGAN MCINERNEY
Jason	ELIOT COLE
Mrs. Marsh	DEANA DUNCAN
June	GAEA VAN BREDA
Chris	RYAN KARAMANYAN
Adelaide	KATRINA ELLISON
Lucy	STEPHANIE METZ
Billy	KEITH KINSEY

CATHY'S CREEK was selected for development at the 2003 Waldo M. and Grace C. Bonderman Playwriting for Youth National Symposium where it received a staged reading at Indiana Repertory Theatre, directed by Christopher Gurr.

CATHY'S CREEK was subsequently produced at Stages Theatre Company in Hopkins, Minnesota, in October 2004. It was directed by Sandy Boren-Barret and associate directed by Bruce Rowan, with set design by Gretchen Katt, costumes by Lori Opsal, lighting by Rob Johnson, props by Jim Hibbeler, and make-up by Paula Lee. The stage managers were Melanie Salmon-Peterson and Kristin Larsen. The music was played by Karen Ouren and Josh Kaplan.

Cathy. . . . . MOLLY DWORSKY & TARA BORMAN
Jeanne . . . . SARA SAWYER
Myrna . . . . MARILEE MAHLER
Mike . . . . THOMAS BEVAN
Jack . . . . BRUCE ROWAN
Jason . . . . MATT OUREN
Mrs. Marsh . . . . ALIA MORTENSEN
Chris. . . . . DEREK PRESTLY
Adelaide . . . . ZOEY SCHULTZ
Inquisitor . . . . BRENT TECLAW

CATHY'S CREEK

A Musical in Two Acts
For 5m., 5w.
(with doubling, 4m. instead of 5) extras as desired

CHARACTERS

CATHY SCRUGGS . . . . female, 13-14 years old
JEANNE D'ARC. . . . . female, 16 years old
MYRNA SCRUGGS. . . . . female, 35-45 years old
JACK DECASTRO . . . . male, 45-55 years old
MICHAEL SCRUGGS . . . . male, 16 years old
CHRIS DECASTRO . . . . male, 13-14 years old
ADELAIDE . . . . female, 13-14 years old
JASON PRITCHARD . . . . male, 13-14 years old
MRS. MARSH . . . . female, 35-55 years old
INQUISITOR (or, an offstage male VOICE, which can be
    sung by the actors playing JASON and/or
    MICHAEL)

THE TIME: Present day.
THE PLACE: A small town in the Iowa farm country.

The action, for the most part, takes place in three locales: by
the banks of Angel Creek, in the dining area and front porch of
Cathy's house, and in Mrs. Marsh's classroom.

I believe the play is best served by a flexible unit set. Much
of the story takes place in Cathy's imagination—thus characters,
both imaginary and real, must be free to enter and exit with the
ease and speed of thought. Clunky and unwieldy scene changes

would slow this down considerably and might distract from Cathy's internal journey.

At the same time, I have to admit, a "real" creek, with actual water, running down the middle of the stage would be great. Stars, for the night scenes, and a big moon would also be lovely. It would be great if there were a tree to climb, or a tire to swing on, and plants...

But a production would also work just fine with a couple of platforms, some sturdy chairs and clever lighting. After all, in the end, this is a play about what happens inside and between people, before they go out and change the world.

SONGS

Hearing Voices . . . . Cathy, Jeanne, Myrna
All You Got Is You. . . . . Jack and Students*
Conversation. . . . . Jeanne, Cathy
Just Sign Your Name. . . . . Jack, Myrna
Telescope . . . . Jason
Argument . . . . Myrna, Cathy
One Girl. . . . . Cathy, Jeanne
Playing to Win . . . . Cathy, Jeanne
End Act I . . . . Jeanne, Cathy, Mike, Jack*, Myrna, Adelaide*
Cathy's Plan . . . . Myrna, Cathy, Jeanne
Stay the Course . . . . Mike, Myrna
Interview/Trial . . . . Inquisitor, Jeanne, Jack, Cathy
Cathy Fragment . . . . Cathy
When You Know the Truth . . . . Mike
Jeanne/Cathy Fragment . . . . Jeanne, Cathy
The Rally . . . . Jack, Jeanne, Cathy*, Myrna*, Townspeople*
Finale. . . . . All

* Speaking parts only, but they are essential to the tune.

ACT ONE

(On one side of the stage, JEANNE, a French farm girl in the Middle Ages. On the other side of the stage, CATHY SCRUGGS, an American farm girl of the present day.)

(MUSIC #1: HEARING VOICES)

CATHY.
> **DO YOU EVER HEAR THINGS?**

JEANNE.
> **I HEAR VOICES...**

CATHY.
> **AND IT SOUNDS AMAZING, AND IT SOUNDS
> LIKE MAGIC**

JEANNE.
> **I HEAR ANGEL VOICES...**

CATHY.
> **AND IF YOU OPEN YOUR MOUTH, 'CAUSE YOU
> WANT 'EM TO KNOW
> NOBODY LISTENS AND THEY TELL YOU TO GO
> AWAY**

JEANNE.
> **I TRY HARD TO LISTEN**

MYRNA *(off. CATHY's mother)*. Who are you talking to
out there?
CATHY *(yelling to MYRNA)*. Nobody!

JEANNE.
> **VOICES…**

CATHY *(in a softer tone)*.
> **DO YOU EVER FEEL THINGS?**
> **LIKE I FEEL THE EARTH**

JEANNE.
> **AND I HEAR VOICES IN THE SKY**
> **GIVING MY SPIRIT BIRTH**

CATHY.
> **PEOPLE THEY THINK I'M CRAZY**
> **PEOPLE DON'T UNDERSTAND**

MYRNA *(speaking off)*. Cathy, I hope you aren't lying in
the grass with your hands in the dirt.

CATHY.
> **BUT I SWEAR I HEAR THE GRASS HUMMING**
> **AND SEEDS SINGING AND SOIL SIGHING**

JEANNE.
> **AND COURAGE RISING AND ARMIES FALLING**
> **AND—**

CATHY & JEANNE.
    VOICES CALLING ME
    TELLING ME THINGS TO KNOW
    TELLING ME THINGS THAT SOMEONE NEEDS
       TO KNOW

CATHY *(yelling off to MYRNA)*. I'm going down to the creek.

MYRNA. Did you finish your homework?

CATHY. Yes.

MYRNA *(entering, a nice-looking woman)*. Your biography research?

CATHY *(waving a book)*. I got it, see? I'll read down there.

MYRNA. Supper's gonna be ready in just a little while.

CATHY. You going out again tonight?

MYRNA. I don't "go out" on weeknights, thank you very much. What's this about? *(CATHY shrugs.)* Don't stay too long, Cathy…and watch who you talk to.

JEANNE.
    I NEED TO KNOW HOW—THE VOICES TELL ME
      LISTEN
    I NEED TO KNOW WHEN
    THE VOICES TELL ME WAIT…

MYRNA.	CATHY.	JEANNE.
LISTEN TO ME NOW	EVERYTHING SEEMS	ANGELS ALL
CATHY, LISTEN HERE	SO HOPELESS NOW	AROUND ME
NO ONE'S EVER		
GONNA PAY YOUR		
WAY THROUGH LIFE		
FEET ON THE GROUND	I REMEMBER WE	MIRACLES ABOUND
NOSE TO THE GRIND-	LAUGHED OUT LOUD	
STONE THAT'S THE		

MYRNA.	CATHY.	JEANNE.
WAY YOU MAKE		
YOUR WAY THROUGH		
LIFE		
WAKE UP TO THIS	IT WAS FUN, WE'D GO	YOU'RE WATCHING
WORLD	TO TOWN	OVER ME
LISTEN TO ME, GIRL	WE WOULD PLAY	YOU'RE WATCHING
	UNTIL SUNDOWN	OVER ME
YOUR PA AND YOUR	NOW I DON'T KNOW	I AM NOT AFRAID
BROTHER BOTH ARE	WHERE I BELONG	AND
GONE; NOTHIN'S EVER		
GONNA BRING THEM		
BACK		
ALIVE FOR US		
NO AMOUNT OF		
DREAMIN'	I USED TO FIT NOW	I AM NOT ALONE
LOOKIN' FOR 'EM	I'M ALL WRONG	
DOWN BY THE CREEK		
BRING 'EM BACK		
ALIVE		
FOR US		
HEAR ME SAY THESE	USED TO COME HERE	YOUR HOLY SPIRIT
WORDS	ALL THE TIME	LEADS
LISTEN TO ME, GIRL	WAS SO HAPPY BUT	YOUR HOLY SPIRIT
	NOW I'M	LEADS
MORTGAGE, TAXES,	FEELING STRANGE	FAITH
RENT	I'M CHANGING	TRUST
YOU WONDER WHERE	I'M SAD	TRIUMPH
THE MONEY WENT		
YOU'RE SPENDING		
EVERY SINGLE CENT	AND IT'S TOO BAD	AND I WILL
THIS IS NOT THE	'CAUSE NO ONE	ALWAYS
LIFE I MEANT	LISTENS TO	LISTEN FOR
FOR US OH PLEASE		
JUST LISTEN TO MY	MY VOICE	YOUR VOICE
VOICE		YOU WILL SHOW ME
		HOW

(JACK, a handsome middle-aged man, appears on stage and hails MYRNA. He approaches and kisses her hand. She walks off the porch. CATHY watches.)

MYRNA. Jack, how wonderful to see you!

(He tucks her arm under his and they exit, as if on a romantic walk at sunset. The rest of MYRNA's song sung as if she is replying to questions and having a conversation with JACK.)

MYRNA.	CATHY.	JEANNE.
OKAY, LET'S GO	MAMA DOESN'T LISTEN	I AM LISTENING
	MAMA DOESN'T HEAR	
BUT DINNER'S	DOESN'T CARE ABOUT	WAITING FOR YOUR
ALMOST READY NOW	A THING THESE DAYS	WISDOM
NEXT WEEK WOULD	GET YOUR HOMEWORK	
BE FINE FOR ME	DONE, DO THE	SHOWING ME
	DISHES	THE WAY
	DID YOU MAKE YOUR	
USED TO GO THERE	BED, THAT'S ALL I	YOU'RE SHOWING
ALL THE TIME THAT	HEAR THESE DAYS	ME THE WAY
WAS BEFORE I WORKED	WISH THAT SHE COULD	
FULL TIME LONG,	SEE, WISH THAT SHE	
LONG AGO...	COULD HEAR	
	WHERE DID SHE GO?	WHEREVER I GO

CATHY *(MYRNA and JACK have exited. She stares after them)*.
    DO YOU EVER HEAR THINGS?

JEANNE.
    I HEAR YOUR VOICE.

(The song has brought them to opposite sides of the creek on a now-emptied stage. They look at one another.)

JEANNE. Are you a holy saint?

CATHY. Who are you?

MIKE *(off)*. Hey, Cathy! *(CATHY and JEANNE both turn their heads.)*

CATHY *(quick, almost desperate)*. You can hear him?

JEANNE. He called you Catherine.

CATHY *(mystified)*. That's Michael, my brother. But how…

JEANNE. St. Michael! And you are Catherine— *(She prostrates herself.)* I am afraid—I am afraid to look upon you.

(She runs from the stage as MIKE enters, a nice-looking young man with a baseball bat.)

CATHY. Mike, this girl can hear you! *(Beat.)* Where did she go?

MIKE. She'll be back.

CATHY. Who is she?

MIKE. You'll find out soon enough. What's the book?

CATHY. Oh, for school. Everyone has to do a biography report. I got Joan of the Ark.

MIKE. Joan of Arc. Been reading it?

CATHY. Sort of. *(MIKE looks at her.)* Um, she lived in France a long time ago? Okay look, I've never been good at reading, Mike, you know that—

MIKE. This book's important, Cathy—

CATHY. Oh, please—you sound just like Mama. "Do your homework, eat your vegetables, pay attention." You know, she's with "him" again, right now? She made this big deal about supper being almost ready, and then he comes waltzing by and boom! She drops everything to go off into the sunset. We'll be eating burned pot roast tonight, I know it.

MIKE. Aw, Cathy—

CATHY. What if she marries him?

MIKE. I don't think that's what's going on. Listen—

CATHY. What do you know about Mama, anymore? She's changed. She doesn't want me coming down here to talk to you. She hates this creek and I think she even hates me sometimes, Mike—

MIKE. Cathy, Mama used to come down here all the time. Taught us how to fish with Wonderbread spitballs and a red bobber on the water. Remember?

CATHY. I can't picture it.

MIKE. No fish in the creek now, anyway.

CATHY. Some of the plants are coming back, though. Solomon seal's there, and some blue phlox—

MIKE. Listen, Cathy—

CATHY *(not paying attention)*. This boy at school, Jason Pritchard? He said phlox was for weaving and heart disease and I told him he had foxglove and flax mixed up, and you should have seen him when I—

MIKE. Cathy. There's something going on with the water and you have to find out what it is.

CATHY. Mike, the creek's been dead ever since—

MIKE. That's not what I mean. Something about the water…it's calling me, real loud. Can you hear it?

CATHY. I just hear you right now.

MIKE. Well, I keep coming back, and looking at it… But that's all I can do. So, I need you to find out some things for me. It's gonna be hard, I think, but I got someone to help—

CATHY. I'll have you know I have a lot on my mind! I have Joan of the Ark to read, and Mama's already on my back about all my other grades—

MIKE. I wouldn't ask you if it wasn't important. What do you say?

CATHY *(sighs. An old saying).* For you the moon, Mike.

MIKE. You're my star, Little Sprout. *(Pause.)* Jason Pritchard, huh?

CATHY. Mike, he's such a jerk!

MIKE. You like him.

CATHY. I do not!

MIKE. Yeah, you do. *(CATHY scoffs.)* You better head up to supper. I think Mama's back from her walk.

CATHY *(gets up).* I wish you could come, too. *(MIKE shakes his head.)* If she could see you—

MIKE. She can't.

CATHY. We sit at the dinner table together and there's this big space between us.

MIKE. She's just…seeing what she thinks she needs to see, Cathy. It doesn't do any good to get mad about it.

CATHY. If she came down here, like I do, and cleared her mind, like I do…would she hear you?

MIKE. If she did, I'd just bug her about the water, too. *(He smiles.)*

CATHY. Oh, fine.

MIKE. See you later. *(He starts to exit.)*

CATHY. Mike? I do like him. Jason Pritchard, I mean.

MIKE. I know.

CATHY. But why? He's not even nice.

MIKE. Think about that creek, the water, all right? *(He exits.)*

CATHY *(yelling after him)*. Mike! I gotta think about my report! You know?

*(Spot on CHRIS DECASTRO, a boy in CATHY's class at school. **MUSIC #2: ALL YOU GOT IS YOU**.)*

CHRIS. My name is Christopher John DeCastro, and I'm doing my report on Jack DeCastro, who is my uncle.
MRS. MARSH *(entering with STUDENTS)*. Chris, what a lovely idea! Your uncle is our local hero.
CHRIS. Yup. He turned my grandad's little farm into one of the biggest egg, chicken and pork factory farms in the whole country.
JACK *(enters)*. I turned the town around!
MRS. MARSH. Jack DeCastro's here! Hello, Mr. De-Castro!
CHRIS. Uncle Jack built a whole processing plant just outside town. So the chickens and hogs grow up here, and get slaughtered and packaged, all in the same place. It's a lot of work, but his big factories get it done.
JACK. I'm an American-made man, boys and girls. Now let me tell you how it all happened…
    LONG TIME AGO, WAY BEFORE TV
    MY DADDY ON MY GRANDPA'S KNEE
    HE HAD A LITTLE FARM, NOTHING SPECIAL,
      JUST A LITTLE
    FARM…PRETTY MUCH LOW KEY
    HE WORKED REAL HARD, THEN HE DIED
    THEN MY DADDY TRIED WORKIN' REAL HARD
      THEN HE DIED
    WELL I NOTICED WE WERE GETTING POORER
      ALL THE TIME

AND MY MAMA HUNG HER HEAD AND CRIED

THAT'S WHEN I REALLY KNEW
THAT ALL YOU GOT IS YOU
DO WHAT-CHA GOT TO DO
'CAUSE ALL YOU GOT IS YOU

WELL I GOT A LITTLE OLDER AND I GOT A
    LITTLE BOLDER
AND I SAVED A LITTLE MONEY ON THE SIDE
I MADE THE RIGHT FRIENDS, IF YOU KNOW
    WHAT I MEAN
AND I TOOK 'EM ALL ALONG FOR THE RIDE
OUTSMARTED MY FOES, AND HIRED MY
    FAMILY
WHILE THE COMPETITION FREAKED AND
    FRIED
MORE HOGS, MORE CHICKENS, AND WE PICK
    'EM OUT AND
CUT 'EM UP AND SEND 'EM OUT NATIONWIDE

YOU CAN COLLECT YOUR DUE
WHEN ALL YOU GOT IS YOU
WATCH THE MONEY COME ON THROUGH
WHEN ALL YOU GOT IS YOU

JACK *(with STUDENTS doing a "response" back-up
routine).*
    NOW I'M A SELF-MADE MAN DOING ALL I CAN
    TO GIVE THIS POPULATION WHAT IT NEEDS
    I BUILT THIS FACTORY FARM ON NOTHIN' BUT
        BRAINS AND CHARM
    AND I NEVER GAVE UP THINKING I'D SUCCEED

> **SO KIDS, HERE'S THE MOST IMPORTANT PART,**
> ** PAY ATTENTION NOW**
> **IT'S REAL CRUCIAL THAT YOU LISTEN TO ME**
> **WORK IS HARD TO FIND AND MONEY'S HARD**
> ** TO MAKE**
> **AND THOSE ARE THE ABC'S**
> **DECASTRO FARMS IS A PLACE WHERE THE**
> ** MONEY AND THE**
> **WORK AND THE HAPPINESS IS**
> **WE OWN HALF THE COUNTY AND WE FEED**
> ** HALF THE COUNTRY**
> **WE'RE THE BEST IN THE FACTORY FARM BIZ**
>
> **GONNA GIVE YOU ONE MORE CLUE**
> **ALL YOU GOT IS YOU**
> **READY FOR A QUICK REVIEW, CLASS?**

ALL.
> **ALL YOU GOT IS YOU!**

MRS. MARSH. What a wonderful report! Thank you for bringing your uncle to class!

ADELAIDE. I loved your report, Chris!

CHRIS. I bet everyone here got someone in their family working for DeCastro Farms.

ADELAIDE. My dad and my cousin Charlie!

JASON. My mom, too.

JACK. Here in Trawling we're all one big, happy family! Remember that, the next time you sit down to a hot chicken dinner. And tell your folks to remember me next month at election time—I'm running for mayor!

MRS. MARSH. That's wonderful news! *(The bell rings.)* Uh, next we'll hear a report from Adelaide and then Jason and then it's Cathy's turn, right? Cathy?

JACK *(on his way out, stops)*. Cathy! You're Myrna Scruggs little girl, aren't you? Well, I am glad to meet you, finally.

CHRIS. Uncle Jack…

JACK. Just a second, son. I been making a special friend of Cathy's mom recently. But it seems like every time I stop by the house, Cathy here's down at Angel Creek.

CHRIS. Aw, jeez…

JACK. We should get to know each other.

CATHY. I guess I'm awful busy.

MRS. MARSH. I'm sorry—Cathy, can I tear Mr. DeCastro away from you a moment?

CATHY. Be my guest.

MRS. MARSH. Mr. DeCastro—may I call you Jack?—

JACK. Cathy—uh— *(He wants her to wait, but CATHY walks off, pretending not to hear, while MRS. MARSH continues chattering.)*

MRS. MARSH *(overlapping)*. I have something only you can help me with. Now, if you don't mind… *(She is leading him off, chattering.)*

JACK *(overlapping)*. Well, of course I want to listen to everyone in Trawling— Uh, Chris…?

(The three of them have exited, and CATHY, alone on stage, almost bumps into JASON.)

JASON *(hand over heart, imitating MRS. MARSH)*. It's so inspiring to have an actual Man in my classroom! Mr.

DeCastro—may I call you Jack—would you come every day and tell us how wonderful you are?

CATHY. Can you believe it?

JASON. I'll tell you one thing. My mom doesn't talk about how great it is working in Jack DeCastro's chicken factory. Everyone knows it's gross and the pay stinks.

CATHY. I don't want to talk about him, Jason.

JASON. Adelaide says his Cadillac's been parked in your driveway almost every day for the past two weeks.

CATHY. And his butt's been parked on our couch or else he's hauling my mom off to the steakhouse for dinner. You would think after what happened with our creek and his factory, he'd be the last man on earth she'd have anything to do with.

JASON. And they're, like, dating or…?

CATHY. You mean, Adelaide doesn't know? *(Scowling deeply.)* I told you, I don't want to talk about it.

JASON. You…you hear about that dance at the end of the month?

CATHY. What dance?

JASON. Never mind. You know what that plant is?

CATHY. Marsh mallow.

JASON. You're playing with me.

CATHY. No, I'm not.

JASON *(laughing)*. Yeah, right. And I'll just pick myself a graham cracker here and then a Milky Way Bar, c'mon, Cathy—

CATHY *(leaving)*. Oh, go stuff yourself, Jason!

JASON. Hey, where you going?

CATHY. To Angel Creek, to go fishing!

JASON. No fish there anymore!

CATHY. Buzz off! *(She goes to the creek, and JASON shrugs and exits. CATHY sits in a huff.)* Thinks he's so smart. *(Looks at her book.)* Okay, Joan of the Arc—let's go. *(Takes a deep breath, opens her book. **MUSIC #3: CATHY READING**. She reads:)* "As the child of peasants in medieval France, Joan of Arc would have had no formal schooling." Cool. "In fact, even at the time of her death, she could not read or write. However, she had a great deal of practical knowledge, from weaving and animal husbandry, to the medicinal uses for a variety of plants"—me and you, Joan.

(JEANNE appears at the other side of the creek. CATHY looks up.)

CATHY. Hey! You came back—

JEANNE *(prostrating herself)*. Holy Saint Catherine. I beg your pardon.

CATHY. What?

JEANNE. You are Saint Catherine, are you not? And I was afraid before, and I ran from you when you called me, but now—

CATHY. Whoa, I didn't call you. Okay? And I'm not a saint, I'm just a girl.

JEANNE. You do not look like a girl.

CATHY. Thanks a lot. Who are you?

JEANNE. I am called Jeanne. But do you not know this?

CATHY. How would I know?

JEANNE. You are one of my holy voices. *(CATHY looks at her, puzzled.)* I have heard voices of angels since I was thirteen years old.

CATHY. I'm not an angel. But I hear voices sometimes, too. Like Michael, my brother…you heard him yesterday, right?

JEANNE. Yes.

CATHY. That's so cool. He…you know, died…two years ago. But when I'm down here, and I clear out my mind, it's like I can still see him and hear him. Like he never went away.

JEANNE. He is not dead to me. He appears a shining young man, with a sword.

CATHY. That's his baseball bat. He was gonna grow up and hit homers for the Twin Cities or Chicago. But then…he got some kind of blood disease. What do your voices talk to you about?

JEANNE. They say I am to restore peace to the kingdom of France. I am to protect the dauphin—the Crowned Prince—and see to his coronation. I have waited almost four years to act, but soon I will ride to meet the prince, and wear armor, and fight for him.

CATHY. You're going to be a knight in armor?

JEANNE. But surely you know about this Do you not know me, Lady Catherine? I am Jeanne D'Arc, and I am to save the king.

CATHY. Jeanne…Jeanne D'Arc? Jeanne—Joan of Arc?

JEANNE. Have you come to give me leave to ride to the dauphin?

CATHY. I don't know! This is really… *(To the air.)* Hey, Mike! Are you doing this?

JEANNE. Are you not a holy messenger?

CATHY. I'm just a girl.

JEANNE. What is this beautiful place where you live, if it is not heaven?

CATHY. This is…Angel Creek.

(MUSIC #4: CONVERSATION)

JEANNE. Ah. You see? God has sent you!
YOU'RE AN ANGEL
FROM THE BLUE

CATHY.
I'M A FARM GIRL…

JEANNE.
I AM TOO
(Puzzled.)
YOU WEAR…BREECHES?

CATHY.
SO WILL YOU
HERE IS A PICTURE THEY DREW OF YOU

JEANNE. You can see me dressed as you? *(They look at one another.)*
WHAT A WONDER

CATHY.
THIS IS WEIRD

JEANNE.
I PRAYED FOR GUIDANCE
AND YOU APPEARED

CATHY.
CAN'T EXPLAIN IT

STILL I FEEL
SURE THAT I'VE MET YOU
AND SURE THAT YOU'RE REAL
HAVE YOU BEEN WITH ME ALL MY LIFE?

JEANNE.
WILL YOU BE WITH ME ALL MY LIFE?
Instruct me, messenger! When do I ride to the dauphin?

CATHY *(looking it up in the book)*. Um. Well. Okay, you have a cousin who's gonna have a baby soon?

JEANNE. Yes.

CATHY. So you tell your folks you got to go visit her. To help with the baby. But when you get to her village you look up a guy called Commander Baudricourt. He'll help you get to the prince.

JEANNE. Thank you, Catherine. *(Memorizing.)* As soon as the baby is born, I will begin.
GOD HAS CHOSEN ME, I MUST GO
MY HEART IS GRATEFUL
FOR THIS I KNOW
HE HAS SENT YOU
TO MY AID
SOMEONE LIKE ME
A GIRL, A FARM MAID

CATHY.
I JUST HOPE THAT
I CAN DO
ALL THE THINGS
YOU NEED ME TO

JEANNE.
> I HAVE WAITED FOR THIS SIGN
> PART OF A SACRED DESIGN
> RIVER OF ANGELS, A FARM UP ABOVE
> PROOF ONCE AGAIN OF GOD'S LOVE
> HAVE YOU BEEN WITH ME ALL MY LIFE?

CATHY.
> WILL YOU BE WITH ME ALL MY LIFE?

(Indicating book.) I see here some people don't believe in your voices. They laugh at mine, too. I'm glad you understand.
> ONLY THING IS
> I CAN'T SAY
> WHAT A NICE TIME I HAD WITH YOU TODAY
> CAN'T YOU SEE IT? "OH, OH, CHRIS—
> ME AND JOAN OF ARC, WE'RE LIKE THIS"

JEANNE.
> WHAT A BLESSING THOUGH, I HAVE YOU

CATHY.
> FEEL LIKE I'VE KNOWN YOU FOREVER TOO
> IS THIS REAL OR JUST PRETEND?
> STILL I CAN CALL YOU MY FRIEND

JEANNE & CATHY.
> HAVE YOU BEEN WITH ME ALL MY LIFE?
> WILL YOU BE WITH ME ALL MY LIFE?

CATHY. Jeanne? Does your mom get mad when you tell her about the voices?

JEANNE. I tell no one of my voices, Catherine. If my father knew what I had been told and what I planned to do, he would disown me, or have me killed.

CATHY. But you listen to them anyway?

JEANNE. I ignore them at my peril. As would you, my lady. What does Saint Michael ask of you, when he comes to you to speak?

CATHY. Mike? Well, lately, he's been talking about— water, but—

JEANNE. This river?

CATHY. I guess so. There's this big hog farm over the hill there, spilled a bunch of manure in the creek a few years back and killed all the fish—

JEANNE. A farmer poisoned the water?

CATHY. Oh, yeah. A…big farmer, like—I guess what you'd call a duke? He's got so many thousands of hogs, they make a lake a manure almost every day. No kidding, it's really gross. And most of the time it's, like, pumped into these pipes and canals, for fertilizer? But back in sixth grade, a pipe broke and something like a million tons of manure spilled all over this place. It killed almost everything down here, and it smelled— well, you know.

JEANNE. No doubt the archangel Michael is angry, because a lord who poisons his people is a false lord, my lady, as the English lords in my land are false. *(As they exit.)* I have some questions regarding this commander you say I must meet…

CATHY. From what I've read, it mostly looks like you got to just march up to him and tell him off, Jeanne.

JEANNE *(exiting)*. I am to "tell off" a large, formidable soldier? God give me strength.

*(Lights shift to MYRNA in the house, with JACK. She is
setting the table, he is diverting her.)*

MYRNA. Was she unfriendly to you, then?

JACK. More like…disengaged.

MYRNA. Well, that's Cathy for you. Always got her head
stuck in the clouds.

JACK. Unlike her practical mother.

MYRNA. Believe it or not, I used to be quite the dreamer
too, once upon a time. But I have to see things for how
they are, now. Have had to, for some time.

JACK. Well, I believe I've made you a very practical offer,
ma'am.

MYRNA. Jack. I've lost too much already. That's something you can't understand—

JACK. I understand more than you think. Myrna. I know
what it is to be poor, and to think you got nothing. To
think you are nothing.

MYRNA. What you're talking about is huge. Huge. Flatten
my house. Pave over my land. This is all I have, all I
have, and you want to use it to expand your factory—

JACK. Our factory, that's part of the deal. You'd be made
a full partner, Myrna. Your land for a partnership in my
company.

MYRNA. I don't know anything about hog farming—

JACK. You know a hell of a lot about zoning laws and
building permits and the new bills on the docket for factory farm expansions—

MYRNA. I do know that.

JACK. And I know you can use the money. *(As MYRNA
scoffs.)* You say Cathy's got learning disabilities…
couldn't she use a tutor? You say she's troubled, talks to

herself. Well, how 'bout if you could afford to get her help? Look. Right now we can get a loan from the federal government—close to three million dollars—to expand the factory over your land here. But we gotta jump on it. *(As she tries to interrupt.)* I could use the loan, the town could use the expansion and you—you and Cathy could use a sea change, Myrna. Don't deny it. I can have my lawyer draw up the papers next week.

MYRNA. I—I can't make up my mind that fast, Jack. There's an awful lot to consider—

(MUSIC #5: JUST SIGN YOUR NAME)

JACK.
> **LISTEN, MYRNA, NOW YOU GOTTA OPEN YOUR MIND**
> **LIFE IS GONNA OPEN UP TO YOU WHEN YOU FINALLY SAY**
> **YOU'RE GONNA COME MY WAY**

MYRNA.
> **WAY TOO FAST, SLOW DOWN**
> **WE NEED SOLID GROUND**

JACK.
> **GROUND YOUR DREAMS IN REALITY**
> **MAKE THEM ALL ACTUALITIES AND LIVE**
> **JUST GIVE YOUR LIFE A CHANCE**

MYRNA.
> **CHANCES ARE THERE'S MORE**

JACK. Give it a chance—

MYRNA.
> **BUT I'VE BEEN WRONG BEFORE**

JACK.
> **BEFORE YOU MAKE UP YOUR MIND...**

MYRNA. Jack, we need to talk, I...

JACK.
> **PLEASE LET ME JUST REMIND YOU**

MYRNA. Wait a minute here...

JACK.
> **YOU WILL HAVE TIME TO SPEND**

MYRNA. Time?

JACK.
> **TIME WITH FRIENDS**

MYRNA. Friends?

JACK.
> **TIME TO BE WITH YOUR DAUGHTER**

MYRNA.
> **MY DAUGHTER**

JACK.
> **TIME JUST TO REST**

MYRNA.
> **OH JACK I'M SO TIRED, I NEED A REST**

JACK.
> **SIT BACK AND I'M MAKING SURE**
> **YOUR LIFE IS THE BEST**

I've gotten where I am by doing, Myrna, not by sitting around thinking. You want more—you gotta take more, and damn the torpedoes.

MYRNA. I don't—

JACK. The potential—for everyone—is almost limitless. You could make that happen, if you just join forces with me.

MYRNA. I…wow, Jack.
> **THE REST OF MY LIFE JUST DOESN'T LOOK SO**
> **   BRIGHT**
> **BUT NOW THERE MIGHT BE JUST A LITTLE**
> **   TINY LIGHT AHEAD**
> **MIGHT WANNA USE MY HEAD**

JACK.
> **HEAD ON OUT WITH ME**
> **COME WITH ME, YOU'LL SEE**

MYRNA.
> **I SEE IT NOW, MY LIFE HAS BEEN SO HARD**
> **BEEN TRYIN' AND TRYIN' TO GET OVER ALL**
> **   THE WOUNDS AND SCARS**
> **BUT NOW THERE'S MOON AND STARS**

JACK.
> **AND FANCY CARS**

MYRNA.
AND SLEEPING IN

JACK.
AND WE BOTH WIN

MYRNA.
COULD BE SO GRAND

JACK.
WITH PEN IN HAND
YOU STAKE YOUR CLAIM
JUST SIGN YOUR NAME

MYRNA.
I'LL THINK ABOUT IT

*(Lights change to CATHY at the creek. **MUSIC #6: TELESCOPE**. It is dark. JASON enters with a telescope.)*

CATHY. Who's there?
JASON. That you, Cathy?
CATHY. Jason? What are you doing at Angel Creek this time of night?
JASON. I was gonna have a look at the sky.
CATHY. That a telescope?
JASON. Yeah. Am I bothering you?
CATHY. Can I look through it?
JASON. After I get it set up. *(He does so, while they talk.)*
CATHY. I didn't know you had a telescope.

JASON. Got a job over the summer. Cleaning pens for Jack DeCastro over at the hog farm.
CATHY. Yuck!
JASON. Yeah, it sucked. But… My dad's been sick, and DeCastro let me help out. Paid me under the table, cash.
CATHY. That was nice.
JASON. It was hard. But I bought this. I like the stars, always have. *(He aims the telescope and lets CATHY look through it at different points in the sky.)*

    FROM FAR AWAY
    THEY LOOK SO SIMPLE
    JUST PRETTY LITTLE LIGHTS IN THE BLACK
    FROM FAR AWAY, THEY'RE ALL THE SAME
    JUST A BUNCH OF WHITE STARS BLINKIN'
        BACK

    BUT LOOK UP CLOSE
    IN THIS TELESCOPE
    I'LL TELL YOU WHAT YOU'RE GONNA FIND
    WORLDS EXPLODING AND GALAXIES
        FLOATING
    AND COLORS OF EVERY SINGLE KIND
    IF YOU NEVER STOP TO LOOK UP CLOSE
(She and JASON make eye contact and look away.)
    YOU'LL MISS THE STUFF THAT YOU WANNA
        SEE THE MOST
    MORNING STAR, EVENING STAR, WISH UPON A
        STAR

    CAMPING WITH MY DAD
    OUT UNDER THE STARS
    HE SHOWED ME HOW TO FIND MY WAY
    AND THAT'S WHY I BOUGHT
    THIS TELESCOPE

WITH SAVINGS FROM MY TAKE-HOME PAY
YOU LOOK UP THERE
THROUGH THE ENDLESS AIR
YOU CAN LOSE YOURSELF IN THAT AMAZING
   PLACE
AND IF YOU KNOW
JUST HOW TO LOOK
THEY CAN TELL YOU WHERE YOU ARE IN
   SPACE

IF YOU NEVER WONDER WHERE YOU ARE
YOU'LL GET SO LOST, YOU WILL LOSE YOUR
   GUIDING STAR
SHOOTING STAR, FALLING STAR, WISH UPON A
   STAR

I WATCH AT NIGHT
AND THRILL AT THE SIGHT
OF SOMETHING SO MUCH BIGGER THAN ME
IT'S SO FAR AWAY
FROM WHAT I DID TODAY
BUT I'M RIGHT THERE IN THAT MYSTERY

IF YOU NEVER STOP TO LOOK UP CLOSE
YOU'LL MISS THE STUFF THAT YOU WANNA
   SEE THE MOST
RISING STAR, LUCKY STAR, WISH UPON A
   STAR
EVENING STAR, MORNING STAR, WISH UPON A
   STAR

CATHY *(looking through the telescope)*. It's not one star at all! It's two!

JASON. That's a binary system.

CATHY. It looks like just one without the telescope.

JASON. They circle around each other. Connected by gravity, or dark matter. Or just because. *(Beat.)* Turns out there is such a thing as a marsh mallow plant.

CATHY. I know.

JASON. I looked it up on the Internet when I got home. The roots taste like candy.

CATHY. So does the sap—

JASON. You were right and I was—

CATHY. A jerk.

JASON. Yeah. *(Beat.)* How come you're out so late?

CATHY. You can see Jack DeCastro's Cadillac in the driveway from here.

JASON. At my house there's nothing but medicine in the refrigerator. And my mom and dad were fighting again so it seemed like a good time to check out.

CATHY. Your dad's real sick, huh?

(MIKE enters and sits quietly by the creek.)

JASON. We don't know if he'll get better. It's funny how he needs so much help, and it's like we're all just—angry about it and fight all the time.

CATHY. That's how it was with Mike.

JASON. I was sorry when he died. I guess I was too embarrassed to tell you that when it happened.

CATHY. That's okay. *(Beat.)* You still working for Mr. DeCastro?

JASON. Not since school started. If I never had to go back there!

CATHY. Is it all horrible?

JASON *(accompanied by appropriate shrieks from CATHY)*. You're closed in with a hundred thousand pigs, Cathy, and, well, the smell in that place is so bad— Your nose and eyes start running from the time you walk in the door. You gotta wear these big, hot rubber boots and rubber gloves, because if you're not stepping in piles and piles of manure, you're slipping in rivers of—

CATHY. Ew! Stop!

JASON. You never really think about manure until you're knee-deep in the stuff all day and then it's like you can't ever really get the taste out of the back of your mouth. There's something wrong with that place. *(MIKE cups his hand to drink from the creek.)*

CATHY *(to MIKE)*. You shouldn't do that!

JASON. Do what?

CATHY. I mean, you shouldn't say that.

JASON. DeCastro is all about cutting corners and making money. His factory's like a crappy little concentration camp, only worse. The cement reservoir he's got to hold all the waste? It's older than me, it's got all kinds of cracks. And the pumping system for the manure pipes— it's made out of aluminum, and dents in a rainstorm—

CATHY. He was supposed to replace all that old stuff after that spill happened down here—

JASON. Yeah, well. He makes a lot of money, Cathy, but he pays out as little as possible—whether it's in bad feed, or bad materials...or underage labor. It's not just me, either. My mom'll tell you stories about the chicken factory that're worse.

CATHY. Someone should shut him down, then.

JASON. You heard Chris's report. The factory shuts down, and you might as well shut down the county.

MIKE. You hear what he's saying?

CATHY *(to MIKE)*. Oh, just be quiet!

JASON. You don't like me much, do you, Cathy?

CATHY. Oh, no! I mean, well—I…wouldn't say I hate you…exactly.

JASON. Most girls, if they're mad at you, they won't let on that they are. They'll act like everything's fine and then they say nasty things behind your back. But I like making you mad because you always let me know. You always tell the truth. I like that.

CATHY. Really? Wow. Because I…well, I like—

MIKE. Cathy, you got to ask about the water.

CATHY *(glaring at him)*. Supposing Jack DeCastro has leaky pipes, or an old cracked reservoir, like you said— would that mean there's more junk being spilled in my creek here?

JASON. Yeah, maybe. But it doesn't really matter, does it?

CATHY. I love this creek and I want the fish to come back

JASON. Well, some people like being warm in the wintertime, or having food on the table—

CATHY. But—

MIKE. Look at the creek, Sprout.

JASON. Boy, it looks simple from far away—

MIKE. Look at it!

JASON. But nothing's simple up close.

MIKE. I want you to pay attention—

CATHY *(to MIKE)*. Go away, okay? Not now!

JASON. Fine! *(He stalks off.)*

CATHY. Wait! I didn't mean you! I meant... *(He is gone. To MIKE who continues to look at her.)* Mike, come on, this is just something Jason Pritchard said, it's not like... I mean, I don't know anything about hog manure, or water, or creeks or...

MYRNA *(off)*. Cathy! Cathy!

CATHY. And I better get home. *(She takes the opportunity to go.)*

MIKE. Don't run away from this. Cathy, I need you.

(He exits as lights change, CATHY at the house.)

MYRNA. Where on earth have you been?

CATHY. What made you totally lose track of time until right now?

MYRNA. Cathy, don't start—

CATHY. He only just left!

MYRNA. That's no reason for you not to come home.

CATHY. Well, I'm not coming home if Jack's here.

MYRNA. Cathy! He's been nothing but charming and kind to—to both of us! What's the matter with you?

CATHY. Is he your boyfriend?

MYRNA. What if he is?

CATHY. Is he?

MYRNA. Not exactly.

CATHY. Then why is he—with—you all the time?

MYRNA. We have some things to talk about. Jack is interested in expanding his hog factory—over—our land. This house and the creek, specifically. If I let him.

CATHY. He wants to—

MYRNA. He'd pay me a lot of money, Cathy. And we could use it. Plus, I'd own part of the factory.

CATHY. But the creek is where Michael and I—I mean, where we used to—

MYRNA. Michael's been dead for more than two years.

CATHY. I know. But— See—

MYRNA. It's not like he's down at the creek right now—

CATHY. Yes, he is. I mean, I know he isn't really, but, Mama, I miss him. I like to go down there, I—

MYRNA. Cathy, it's not good for you to live in another world like this—

CATHY. I'm not. I'm— I just— How—how come you don't like to hear about Michael, don't you miss him too, because if you did you might—

MYRNA. We both have to move on. Dammit, Cathy. I'm talking about a new life for us here and you're... I'm worried about you when you talk about Michael like he's down there swinging a bat. He's not! And Jack's made a very solid proposal—

CATHY. Jack ruined our creek! His factory killed all the fish and—

MYRNA. He's very sorry about that, really he is—

CATHY. Everyone says his factory's disgusting and he cuts corners, Mama! He pays the people who work for him really low wages and it's—

MYRNA. Oh, you don't know anything about this—

CATHY. I do! If you owned the factory, too, you'd be like him, some money-grubbing, greedy old polluter, who—

MYRNA. Cathy, stop it! Right now!

CATHY. No!

(MUSIC #7: ARGUMENT)

MYRNA.
   YOU THINK YOU KNOW THE WORLD

CATHY.
YOU THINK I DON'T?

MYRNA.
YOU THINK YOU KNOW THE TRUTH

CATHY.
I DO!

MYRNA.
AND IN YOUR YOUTH

CATHY.
OH, HERE WE GO

MYRNA.
YOU THINK THE WORLD IS CUT AND DRIED

CATHY.
WELL?

MYRNA.
BLACK AND WHITE

CATHY.
YOUR POINT?

MYRNA.
EITHER WRONG OR RIGHT

CATHY.
YOU USED TO WALK DOWN BY THE CREEK

MYRNA.
> **THOSE DAYS ARE GONE**

CATHY.
> **YOU USED TO TAKE US TO THE CREEK**

MYRNA.
> **CATHY, MOVE ON**

CATHY.
> **TELL US STORIES**
> **JUMP IN AND SWIM**
> **BUT NO. NOW YOU'RE WITH HIM.**

MYRNA.
> **I DON'T KNOW YOU ANYMORE**
> **YOU'RE ALWAYS OVER THERE**

(Indicates creek.)

CATHY.
> **I DON'T KNOW YOU ANYMORE**

I can't believe it…the creek, and you don't care?

MYRNA.
> **THE CREEK IS A SAD PLACE**
> **AND WE NEED TO BUILD**
> **WHAT'S LEFT OF OUR LIVES**
> **WE NEED TO OPEN UP OUR HEARTS**

CATHY.
> **YOU MEAN TO JACK?**

MYRNA.
I MEAN WE NEED A BRAND NEW START
'CAUSE MICHAEL'S NEVER COMING BACK

CATHY.
I WON'T FORGET HIM

MYRNA.
BUT, HONEY, YOU CAN LET HIM
GO...STOP PRETENDING

CATHY. I'm not pretending anything! You don't understand. *(She slams out of the house.)*

MYRNA.
SHE NEEDS TO CHANGE, THAT MUCH IS CLEAR
I'VE HAD IT UP TO HERE
I WILL NOT CRY ANOTHER TEAR
IT'S BEEN SO MANY YEARS SINCE I WAS
    HAPPY
OR SINCE SHE LAUGHED
A BIG OL' DRAFT OF CLEAN FRESH AIR
WOULD DO US GOOD
AT LEAST IT COULD IF SHE WOULD JUST
    WAKE UP!
I AM THE MOTHER HERE. LIFE ISN'T FREE
SHE DOESN'T SEE SOME THINGS THAT I CAN
    SEE
AND I CAN SEE THAT SHE NEEDS MORE
THAT'S WHAT THIS WHOLE FIGHT IS FOR
I WON'T GIVE UP. I'LL STAND MY GROUND
She'll come around…

*(By the end of the song, the lights have changed. CATHY
stands outside in the darkness.)*

CATHY. I don't even have anywhere to go.

JEANNE *(enters, wearing splendid armor)*. Lady
Catherine! It is as you said! I have seen the prince, and
he has given me permission to rescue the town of Orleans!

CATHY. Hey, yeah. I—got that far in the book, too.

JEANNE. Lady Catherine, shall I win this battle?

CATHY. Well. Sure. You're gonna be amazing, Jeanne.
You'll be shot, though—

JEANNE. I will be wounded.

CATHY *(leafs through book to check)*. In the shoulder. But
don't worry. You'll live just fine. Thing is, you have to
keep fighting. After they take the arrow out—you have
to get back up on your horse and make sure the troops
see you're alive. It's seeing you come to life—riding on
your horse after getting, like hurt and all—that gives
your soldiers the final kinda push to win the battle.

JEANNE. An arrow...

CATHY *(showing her the place)*. All the way through.
But—you'll be great. It says so right here.

JEANNE. I thank you for your words of wisdom and advice, Lady Catherine. But why do you look so sad?

CATHY. I can't seem to do one thing right in this world. I
think Michael really does want me to take on—

JEANNE. The poisonous duke?

CATHY. Yeah, him. And if I do...well, everyone I know
will be against me.

JEANNE. Anon, I fight for the prince of France, against
the English army. God has asked this of me, Catherine,

and I must not refuse, though it seems utter folly. We are birds of the same flock, you and I.

CATHY. I'm not like you. Look at you, Jeanne.

JEANNE. Is my armor not splendid? And the prince has presented me with a holy sword and a fine white horse!

CATHY. Do you know how to fight?

JEANNE. No! I am a farm girl. But God will guide my hand, as you have guided my strategy. Will you fight tomorrow too, Lady Catherine?

(MUSIC #8: ONE GIRL)

CATHY.
**I AM ONLY ONE GIRL
I AM ONLY ONE, I CAN ONLY DO SO MUCH
I AM ONLY ONE GIRL
WITH MY ONLY ONE VOICE THAT CAN ONLY
UNDO SO MUCH
THERE'S SO MUCH TO UNDO**

JEANNE.
**BUT ONE GIRL CAN CHANGE THE WORLD
YES ONE GIRL CAN CHANGE THE WORLD**

CATHY. Yeah, but
**THIS IS BIGGER THAN ME
THERE ARE THINGS GOING ON THAT I DON'T
EVEN KNOW ABOUT
I AM ONLY ONE GIRL
IN A WORLD FULL OF GROWNUPS THAT HAVE
IT ALL FIGURED OUT
AND I AM FULL OF DOUBT**

JEANNE.
   BUT ONE GIRL CAN CHANGE THE WORLD
   YES ONE GIRL CAN TAKE TOMORROW BY THE
     HAND
   UNDERSTAND WHAT IT TAKES TO BRING
     SOME PEACE INTO THIS LAND
   TO TAKE A STAND

(MIKE enters and stands with CATHY.)

JEANNE *(cont'd)*.
   WE MAY THINK WE'RE ALONE
   WE MAY THINK WE HAVE ONLY OUR ONE
     SMALL LIFE TO LIVE
   BUT THIS IS BIGGER THAN US
  You're right.
   WE'VE GOT TO STAY WIDE AWAKE,
   THERE ARE MANY MORE LIVES AT STAKE
   AND BRAVE STEPS YET TO TAKE
   AND THIS GIRL CAN CHANGE THE WORLD
(She holds out her hand but CATHY does not take it.)

MIKE. What do you say, Sprout?
CATHY. Is there anyone to help me? Anyone alive I mean?
MIKE. You'd best look to who's close to you.
JEANNE. You must begin with the river.
CATHY. And then what? What do I do then?

(And she looks at the water as the lights change and we find ADELAIDE and the STUDENTS and MRS. MARSH. ADELAIDE is giving her report.)

ADELAIDE. And so, the river song that Pocahontas was singing came true—there really were changes for her. Because she fell in love. And it was love that made Pocahontas stop the war between the Indians and the colonists. She loved John Smith after they sang this song together? And that is why white people are still in America.

MRS. MARSH. Is that the end of your report, Adelaide?

ADELAIDE. That's it.

MRS. MARSH. Can I ask what your sources for your report on Pocahontas were?

ADELAIDE. I read a paragraph in the encyclopedia. But mostly, I watched the movie.

MRS. MARSH. I see.

ADELAIDE. They really fell in love, Mrs. Marsh. It was Meant, you know? And love—it can conquer anything. I mean, John Smith and Pocahontas didn't even speak the same language, but they could understand each other because they were meant for one another. The right person can change everything for someone else, and make everything better. You know what I mean, Chris?

CHRIS. Huh?

MRS. MARSH. Thank you, Adelaide. You may sit down.

ADELAIDE. Okay. *(She sits down after giving CHRIS a big wink.)*

MRS. MARSH. And next week we hear from Jason. And then Cathy? Very well. Let's move on. I'm pleased to introduce a new unit to all of you today. Thanks to Chris's wonderful uncle Jack, I got a memo through to the city council. We will begin following the local elections very closely. It should be tremendously inspiring, as well as educational. Now, you work in teams of two and each team will be assigned a candidate to follow, right up until the election, at which time you will submit your projects for final review.

ADELAIDE. That sounds like a lot of work.

CHRIS. Well, I know who I'm gonna do.

MRS. MARSH. Christopher, you will be working with Cathy—

CATHY. What?

MRS. MARSH *(continuing over)*. Both of you will be following and reporting on your uncle's campaign—

CHRIS *(overlapping)*. With Cathy, wait, but—

MRS. MARSH *(passing out papers)*. Now, we must all learn cooperation and teamwork, that's an essential element to a good education. You have to go with what life hands you—

CHRIS & CATHY *(looking at paper)*. Hold on, I, this isn't what, etc. *(A bell rings.)*

MRS. MARSH. Ah. That will be all for today. If you have questions, see me now. *(STUDENTS file out. CHRIS argues briefly with MRS. MARSH about his project. ADELAIDE stops CATHY.)*

ADELAIDE *(furious)*. Are you inviting him to the Sadie Hawkins dance too, Cathy?

CATHY. What?

ADELAIDE. Dance, hello? At the end of the month? I was going to ask Christopher, but it looks like you have dibs on him in all sorts of ways—

CATHY. Oh, please. Adelaide if you want to ask Chris to a dance, be my guest—

ADELAIDE. I will. Don't worry, I don't need your permission. He'll go with me, too.

CATHY. I hope he does.

ADELAIDE. Let's go, Christopher. *(CHRIS has given up arguing with MRS. MARSH, and turns to CATHY, accusation on his face. They exit, rolling eyes, muttering.)*
CATHY. Mrs. Marsh. I can't do this project—
MRS. MARSH. Cathy, for some reason, Mr. DeCastro has taken a very, shall we say, personal interest in you and requested that you be assigned to his campaign. I should think you would be grateful to be given such an easy assignment.
CATHY. But I—
MRS. MARSH. Do I need to remind you about your grades?
CATHY. I...I don't know what to say.
MRS. MARSH. Say "thank you." Count your blessings. *(She exits.)*
CATHY. Mike, what am I supposed to do now?

(MIKE enters.)

MIKE. You use the opportunity. You study up on De-Castro's farm. You can find out all the—
CATHY. I don't know the first thing about studying. You were the one who was good at school. I'm the dummy, remember?
MIKE. Cathy. Studying is like...baseball. You got to practice and you'll start getting better. You think I started out pitching no-hitters?
CATHY. Yes.

(She picks up her book as JEANNE enters, bandaged but elated.)

JEANNE. Holy St. Michael! Lady Catherine!

CATHY. Jeanne! Are you all right?

JEANNE. But of course. It was a victory at Orleans, as you told me! Lady, my people have outdone themselves in courage and daring.

CATHY. Were you scared?

JEANNE. I was terrified! But it was glorious. A seven-month siege ended! And I! On a white horse, with a flag! The English do not know what to make of me.

CATHY. Says in my book next you have to go and get that prince of yours crowned king…

JEANNE. At Reims, as is the holy tradition. Yes, I will make that my next mission. Thank you, Catherine. And you? How fares the River of Angels and the Evil Duke?

CATHY. Well, it's tricky. I have to—to join forces with a boy I don't trust and—

JEANNE. Raise an army and lay siege to the duke's castle—

CATHY. Sort of. Only I—

JEANNE. Catherine, have no fear. *(MUSIC #9: PLAYING TO WIN.)* If a peasant girl may have regular discourse with the king of France, why then, you need only take your first step—and your task is nearly done.

CATHY. One step? I… Well…well…

I MUST GO WHERE I NEVER HAVE GONE
I MUST DO WHAT I NEVER HAVE DONE
I'M BEGINNING TO MAKE A PLAN
I'M BEGINNING TO THINK…OH, MAN
I'M BEGINNING TO THINK I CAN

JEANNE.
I MUST SAY WHAT I NEVER HAVE SAID

    PUT MY FEET WHERE BRAVE MEN WILL NOT
      TREAD
    I MUST TRY WHAT I'VE NEVER TRIED
    'CAUSE I FEEL SUCH A FIRE INSIDE
    AND SUCH CONFIDENCE IN MY STRIDE

CATHY & JEANNE.
    IT SHOULD FEEL MUCH STRANGER
    TO BE AS STRONG AS THIS
    TO FACE THE REAL DANGERS
    THE RIVALS AND THE RISKS

JEANNE. The road to Reims is long, Catherine. Shall I see the dauphin all the way safely?

CATHY. You fight again at Jar-jee-ow and Pay-tay, but everything comes out fine. You'll be a hero, Jeanne.

MIKE. And Cathy's going to the library—

CATHY. Eesh. Can't I just fight a war, too?

MIKE. Let's go… *(He begins loading her up with books and a pen and eventually she actually sits at a desk and tentatively takes notes.)*

JEANNE.
    AT JARGEAU AND PATAY WE PREVAIL
    THESE ARE VICTORIES ON A GRAND SCALE
    AND THE ARROWS THEY HAVE NO STING
    AND THE PEOPLE THEY KISS MY RING
    BUT I'M JUST UNDER GOD'S GREAT WING

CATHY.
    I DON'T KNOW WHY I WAS SO AFRAID
    WHAT A DIFFERENCE THIS GOOD FRIEND HAS
      MADE

I CAN WALK RIGHT UP TO A BOOK
I CAN READ IT AND SAY, "HEY LOOK!"
I KNOW SOMETHING THAT MAKES THE GRADE

CATHY & JEANNE.
I CAN FEEL MY COURAGE
IT'S COURSING THROUGH MY VEINS
I CAN SEE MY PURPOSE
IT'S CLEAR, IT'S CLEAN AND PLAIN

(As JASON enters.)

JASON. You're in the library, Cathy?

CATHY. Um…

JEANNE. Go on, Catherine! If I can strategize battles with the cream of France's knighthood, you may talk to a boy.

CATHY. I'm doing research, Jason. I'm preparing for my candidate interview with Jack DeCastro.

JASON *(looking at her stack of stuff)*. Uh, this is a magazine about frogs.

CATHY. I know what it is! *(She snatches it back.)* I'm not stupid, okay? This article's about factory farm pollution—like Jack DeCastro's manure spill—and it affects a lot more than creeks, I'll have you know.

JASON *(teasing her)*. Yeah, like frogs…

CATHY. It can mess up groundwater, which is pretty serious, Jason—look.

JASON *(checking it out)*. Wow, okay. *(Reading.)* Listen, I can check some of this stuff out on my dad's computer—see what might be on the Net.

CATHY. You'll help me?

JASON. Yeah. This is amazing, Cathy. *(He exits.)*
CATHY. Jeanne. I'm amazing.

JEANNE.
IT'S AMAZING THE THINGS YOU CAN DO

CATHY.
IT'S AMAZING THE THINGS I CAN DO

JEANNE.
**AND A STRONG FAITH WILL CARRY YOU
THROUGH**

CATHY & JEANNE.
**YOU CAN GO WHERE YOU'VE NEVER BEEN
AND YOU MIGHT TAKE IT ON THE CHIN
BUT YOU KNOW YOU WILL NOT GIVE IN
'CAUSE YOU'RE PLAYING THIS TIME TO WIN
YES, YOU'RE PLAYING THIS TIME TO WIN
WE ARE PLAYING THIS TIME TO WIN**

JEANNE. Our army is unstoppable, Catherine!
CATHY. We are unstoppable, Jeanne!
JEANNE. I could not have done it without your help.

(As CHRIS enters.)

CATHY. Chris…
CHRIS. What's this stuff?
CATHY. It's—uh—my part of our project. I'm getting
　　ready for the—
CHRIS *(leafing through)*. This isn't about the elections.
CATHY. Sure it is. See, I've been looking at—

CHRIS. The Sierra Club! That's some bunny-hugger magazine—

CATHY. Well it monitors the environment and your uncle is—

(As MRS. MARSH enters.)

CHRIS. Mrs. Marsh! I told you she'd mess this up! Look at this—

MRS. MARSH. Do I need to remind you both this is a library?

CHRIS. Well, she's messing up our project. *(He hands her some of CATHY's papers.)*

MRS. MARSH. Chris have a little… *(Looks at them.)* Cathy, what is all this here about water pollution? That isn't even an issue in the election.

CATHY. Well, but remember when that pipe burst by my creek and Mr. DeCastro's factory—

MRS. MARSH. Chris, excuse us. *(To CATHY.)* Cathy, this is not the assignment we discussed. You should be planning to ask your candidate pertinent questions about his platform. Taxes, police and fire budgets…and here you have been researching, well—

CHRIS. Manure. She's reading about manure.

CATHY. Shut up, Chris.

MRS. MARSH. Did you even look at the outline I assigned?

CATHY. Yeah, but see, if Mr. DeCastro expands his factory—

MRS. MARSH. Cathy, this is not acceptable—

CHRIS. That's right, it frickin' blows—

CATHY. Mrs. Marsh, I swear, see, part of his platform is the—

MRS. MARSH. That's it. I'm going to have to call your mother. Clearly I'm not getting through to you about my expectations. Christopher, come with me.

CATHY *(following her, as she exits with CHRIS)*. This really has to do with the election! Mrs. Marsh. Don't call my mom, please? *(To JEANNE.)* That wasn't supposed to happen!

JEANNE. All is not well for me, either. The prince's advisors are jealous of my victories. They vie against me for his favors and whisper lies in his ears.

CATHY. Don't worry. You get to Reims all right and the prince is made king, even though his stupid advisors try to slow him down…

JEANNE. Your assurance brings comfort, but still I don't understand why he insists on these delays.

(MUSIC #10: END ACT I)

WITH WHOM DO THEY THINK I'M ALLIED?
DO I NOT FIGHT WITH GOD ON MY SIDE?
IT SEEMS CLEAR WHERE WE OUGHT TO GO

CATHY.
BUT IT'S LIKE NO ONE WANTS TO KNOW…

(MYRNA enters and crosses to JACK, who has a sheaf of papers.)

JEANNE. Lately, despite my victories, I am overcome with foreboding. Catherine, does some terror await?

(ADELAIDE crosses to CATHY.)

ADELAIDE. Cathy, I heard Jack DeCastro's, like, making your mom some kind of a manager over at the hog factory…?

CATHY. I got some forebodings myself.

JEANNE. The English gather their forces in Paris.

CATHY. I knew I couldn't do this.

MIKE. You got to keep trying for me, Cathy.

ADELAIDE. So how come she gets such a cush job, when she hasn't even worked for him before?

CATHY *(looks at JACK and MYRNA)*. She has something he wants…

JEANNE. The king refuses to let me strike, and treachery seems imminent.

MIKE. You have to tell Mama, Cathy. About the groundwater and what you've found out—

CATHY. She's about to sign over our house, Mike!

ADELAIDE. Cathy, is Mr. DeCastro in love with her or something? I mean, why else would he hire her?

MIKE. You have to speak up!

JEANNE. Catherine, what ought I to do next?

CATHY. I'll see what the book says.

MIKE. Cathy, come on!

**YOU MUST GO WHERE YOU NEVER HAVE
GONE**

JACK. Sometimes you just got to damn the torpedoes, Myrna.

MIKE.

YOU MUST DO WHAT YOU NEVER HAVE DONE

MYRNA. It's a big decision, Jack.
JACK. Just two words.

JEANNE.
  I MUST SAY WHAT I NEVER HAVE SAID
  PUT MY FEET WHERE BRAVE MEN WILL NOT
    TREAD

JACK. Two words.
CATHY *(looking it up in her book)*. Oh, Jeanne!

JEANNE.
  I FALL?

CATHY *(nods)*. The English.
JACK. Say them. *(Silence. Then.)*

MYRNA.
  I WILL!

JACK. Say them loud.
JEANNE *(softly)*. The English.
MYRNA. I will. *(They shake hands and hug.)*
CATHY. Oh, Jeanne.
JEANNE *(as lights go down on JACK and MYRNA)*. I am
  captured by the English? This is God's will?
CATHY. But I'm sure…it's only temporary.

JEANNE.
  THE KING WILL PAY RANSOM OF COURSE
  HE'S GIVEN ME MEN OF VALOR, A SWORD AND
    A HORSE

CATHY.
> **YOU COULD NEVER HAVE COME THIS FAR**
> **JUST TO END UP BEHIND THOSE BARS**

Jeanne, I know it will be fine. Everything's going to be fine. Don't give up.

JEANNE. I shall not, Lady Catherine. By heaven, I fear this with all my heart. *(JEANNE is worried and in tears as she exits.)*

CATHY. Mike, it's going to be all right, isn't it?

MIKE. You have your own job to do.

CATHY. I'm really scared.

END OF ACT ONE

ACT TWO

(MYRNA and CATHY at home. CATHY is waiting on the porch for JACK to show up for his interview and MYRNA is bustling around.)

(MUSIC #11: CATHY'S PLAN)

MYRNA.
    CATHY.

CATHY.
    YEAH?

MYRNA.
    MRS. MARSH CALLED

CATHY.
    SO?

MYRNA.
    SHE SAYS YOU'VE GOT SOME
    INTERVIEW QUESTIONS FOR
    JACK...THAT ARE REALLY
    BUT REALLY OFF TRACK

CATHY.
    I FIXED THEM

MYRNA.
  CATHY.

CATHY.
  I FIXED THEM!

MYRNA.
  CAN I SEE THEM?

CATHY.
  THE NOTEBOOK IS THERE
  ON THE TABLE
  I DON'T KNOW WHY YOU
  DON'T THINK I'M ABLE—

MYRNA.
  I DO

CATHY.
  TO DO THIS

MYRNA.
  I DO, BUT SO WHY DID YOUR TEACHER CALL?
  (CATHY shrugs as MYRNA reads.)
  CATHY, THESE LOOK FINE

CATHY.
  I KNOW
  (Aside.)
  THEY'RE JUST NOT THE ONES
  I'M GONNA ASK HIM TODAY

MYRNA.
 WHA'D'YOU SAY?

CATHY.
 OH, NOTHING.
 JUST THAT I HOPE THIS
 INTERVIEW GETS ME AN "A"

MYRNA.
 CATHY—

(Her question regarding the laundry is inaudible as lights come up on JEANNE.)

JEANNE.
 CATHERINE, HELP ME
 EVERY NIGHT IN THIS COLD CELL
 I DROP DOWN ON MY KNEES
 EVERY DAY I PRAY TO KNOW
 WHICH WAY TO GO, OH PLEASE
 CATHERINE, HELP ME

(CATHY turns to answer but MYRNA's voice has reasserted itself.)

MYRNA.
 OH YES AND THE LAUNDRY!
 IT WAS STILL HERE THIS MORNING
 WHY IS THAT?

CATHY. I forgot. I'm sorry.

MYRNA.
>   **LISTEN!**

JEANNE.
>   **HEAR ME!**

MYRNA. Cathy, listen to me.

JEANNE.
>   **HEAR MY PRAYER!**

MYRNA.
>   **I CAN SEE WHY YOUR TEACHER**
>   **IS STARTING TO WORRY**
> *(A phone rings.)*
>   **I'LL BE BACK IN A MINUTE SO HURRY**

(She exits, still issuing instructions to CATHY, which have become inaudible for the moment.)

JEANNE.
>   **MAKE HASTE**
>   **GUIDE THY SERVANT**
>   **MY COURAGE FAILS**
>   **AND DARKNESS PREVAILS**

CATHY *(quickly, so MYRNA can't catch her talking to JEANNE).*
>   **I'D TELL YOU WHAT TO DO, IF ONLY I KNEW**
>   **BUT YOU HAVE GOT TO FIND YOUR OWN WAY**
>   **THROUGH**
>   **I HAVE SOMETHING REALLY HARD TO DO**
>   **AND I JUST CANNOT BE THERE FOR YOU, TOO**

JEANNE. Catherine, please!

MYRNA *(enters)*.
CATHY, ARE YOU DONE YET?

CATHY.
NOT QUITE

MYRNA.
**OH COME ON, THIS IS
NOT SOMETHING THAT TAKES ALL DAY
DID YOU DO IT THE WAY I SHOWED YOU?**

JEANNE.
HELP ME, CATHERINE!

CATHY.
I CAN'T!

MYRNA.
**OH, YOU CAN'T, WELL THAT'S
REALLY TOO BAD 'CAUSE YOU HAVE TO
I AM SO SICK OF YOU BEING HALF HERE**

JEANNE.
**CATHERINE, PLEASE HELP ME!
CATHERINE!**

MYRNA. Cathy! Snap out of it!
CATHY. I'm sorry!
MYRNA. What's the matter with you?
JEANNE. Catherine. Why has the king not paid my ran-
som?

CATHY. I can't—

JEANNE. The English have called me a witch! They will put me on trial. What is to become of me?

CATHY. Leave me alone! *(Lights out on JEANNE.)*

MYRNA. Cathy, how dare you!

CATHY. I'm sorry!

MYRNA. Well excuse me if I don't believe that!

CATHY. I—I guess I'm just freaked out.

MYRNA. That is the first thing you've said this morning that makes any sense at all. *(Looks at her watch.)* Jack's going to be here with Chris for that interview any minute and I haven't even looked at those papers he gave me to sign.

CATHY. Chris is coming?

MYRNA. Well, aren't you supposed to be working on this project together? *(As phone rings.)* Why do they all got to call on a Saturday morning?

(Exits as MIKE enters.)

CATHY. What am I going to do now?

MIKE. You have to ask him about his factories and the water—

CATHY. With Chris right there? Oh, please.

MIKE. Cathy you're so close...

CATHY. Mama's gonna hate me, I'm gonna flunk school, Chris'll tell everyone about this and everyone at school will laugh—

MYRNA *(off)*. Cathy, there's a boy on the phone. Should I tell him you're busy?

MIKE. I need you to help me—

CATHY. I'm lying to her—

MIKE. You don't have to lie. Who says you have to lie? You just have to—
MYRNA *(off)*. Did you hear me?
CATHY *(she has not)*. It's fine, Mama.
MYRNA *(off)*. Okay.
CATHY. What else am I supposed to do? She's all but sold our house to that—
MIKE. Cathy, you are my eyes and voice. Without you, I'm—I only have this—need to know what's in the water, what's in the—
MYRNA *(entering)*. Do I know Jason Pritchard?
CATHY. What?
MIKE. Cathy—please—you have to do—
MYRNA *(at the same time)*. That boy on the phone—do I know him?
CATHY. Jason— When, when did he call?
MYRNA. I just told you he was on the phone. Where were you?

(MUSIC #12: STAY THE COURSE)

CATHY. I—shoot!
MIKE. If you don't find out about the water—
MYRNA. Is this a special boy?
CATHY. No. I don't know. No!

MIKE.
BE MY MOUTH

MYRNA. You're certainly riled.

MIKE.
   BE MY EYES

MYRNA. There's a lot for you to take in…

MIKE.
   **SPEAK THE TRUTH
   NOT THE LIES**

MYRNA.	**MIKE.**
YOU SWEEP AWAY THE DUST AND DIRT	STAY THE COURSE
	STRAIGHT AND STRONG
AND ALL THE OLD DEBRIS, YOU SEE	YOU'VE KNOWN HOW
CATHY, WE COULD BE FREE	ALL ALONG
IT MIGHT BE PAINFUL NOW	
BUT CATHY, THIS IS HOW IT GOES	
DON'T YOU TURN YOUR BACK	DON'T YOU TURN YOUR BACK
YOU KNOW WHAT TO DO	YOU KNOW WHAT TO DO
I'LL BE THERE FOR YOU	I'LL BE THERE FOR YOU
YOU CAN SEE THIS THROUGH	YOU CAN SEE THIS THROUGH
THIS IS THE BEGINNING OF	
SO MANY THINGS WE'VE WANTED	
AND NOW WE'VE GOT A BREAK	
IT MAY NOT COME AGAIN	
YOU TAKE WHAT YOU CAN TAKE	
I GET THAT THIS IS HARD	STAY THE COURSE
I'M WITH YOU ALL THE WAY	STRAIGHT AND STRONG
HONEY, DON'T YOU SEE	YOU'VE KNOWN HOW
IT'S A BRAND NEW DAY	ALL ALONG
DON'T YOU TURN YOUR BACK	DON'T YOU TURN YOUR BACK
YOU KNOW WHAT TO DO	YOU KNOW WHAT TO DO
I'LL BE THERE FOR YOU	I'LL BE THERE FOR YOU
YOU CAN SEE THIS THROUGH	YOU CAN SEE THIS THROUGH

CATHY. Mama. Listen, I…I found out some things when I
   was researching—

JACK *(entering suddenly)*. Hey there. How are my two girls?

MYRNA *(jumping to attention)*. Jack! You caught us finishing our chores. I'm afraid I haven't looked through those papers you gave me.

JACK. Aw, I'm not here for papers, I'm here for Cathy. Right, kiddo?

CATHY. Hi.

MYRNA. Well, I'll have a look at them while you guys do your work and then… Maybe we can have a talk when you're done? *(She smiles and starts to exit.)* Oh. Was there something you wanted to talk about, Cathy? Your report? *(CATHY shakes her head, MYRNA exits.)*

CHRIS. This sure is a small house.

JACK. Why don't we sit here on the porch. Goodness, you look so serious Cathy, I'm not on trial, am I?

(CATHY has extracted a pad of questions from a secret hiding place. She takes a deep breath and a light comes up on JEANNE, who answers the INQUISITOR as her trial commences. Note: the INQUISITOR can also be a distorted, amplified offstage VOICE, done by the actor playing JASON or MIKE.)

CATHY. No, not you. *(She starts to ask a question and is interrupted by the trial.)*

INQUISITOR. Let's begin with some simple questions. Where do your voices come from? *(MUSIC #13: IN-TERVIEW/TRIAL.)*

JEANNE. Why, from God of course.

JACK. What have you got for me, Cathy? *(Having readied her notes, CATHY prepares to ask a question.)*

CATHY. My uh, my first question, uh, has to do with, um,
    your economic platform…you have a plan to—to ex-
    pand your factory, right here, to help—
JACK. Infuse more revenue in the town. Yes, I do.
CATHY. Uh, revenue?
CHRIS. Money, Cathy. Duh.
CATHY. Um, you say if you expand the factory, there will
    be more jobs…
JACK. It's not rocket science, hon. Anyone can see an ex-
    panded factory's gonna help the local economy.
CATHY. But—um, what about waste facilities?
INQUISITOR. How dare you ask a question! We ask the
    questions, here, not you.
JACK. Waste?
CHRIS. I knew it. I told you.
INQUISITOR. We suspect the devil is your master, child—
JACK. Okay, I'll say this once and for all, and we'll just
    quit, Cathy.
JEANNE. I do not know the devil, I swear it.
JACK. Christopher told me you were researching factory
    farm pollution. I want you to know my factories are in
    complete compliance with the current Clean Water Act
    standards issued by the state.
CATHY. Well but, those standards were made years ago.
    They're out of date, and with so many more hogs, sir—
    the, the waste lagoon you've got—

<table>
<tr><td>CHRIS.</td><td>INQUISITOR.</td></tr>
<tr><td>Cathy, what do you know about—</td><td>You are a child—</td></tr>
</table>

CATHY. Waste lagoon you've got is old and there's better
    ways to—

CHRIS.
What do you know about waste lagoons— Uncle Jack, she's not even in 4-H—

INQUISITOR.
Why would God ask a child to lead an army—

CATHY.
Shut up, Chris!

JEANNE.
I know not the why only that he did—

JACK.
Cathy.

CHRIS. This doesn't have anything to do with the election! He said so!

CATHY. See—everything's related. It's all mixed up together. The water, the plants, the hogs, the air, the town.

JACK.
Is there a question in there, honey?

INQUISITOR
What do you have to say for yourself?

CATHY. If—if you expand the factory, it might really—it might really—mess things up more than they— Hold on. Wait! I'll show you—I drew a chart— *(Looking frantically through the papers.)*

INQUISITOR. We await your answer.

JACK. Whoa, honey, sounds like you're the one mixed up, here.

CHRIS. Amen.

INQUISITOR. It's clear you're confused—

CATHY. It's here somewhere—

INQUISITOR. Possessed—

JEANNE. Test me if you will, you will see I know nothing of demons.

CATHY. See, we need to make sure this expansion is safe or else everything in the whole town could get—hold on…

JACK. Chris, I think maybe I need to talk to Cathy alone?

CHRIS. It's my report, too.

JACK. Just give me a second, okay? *(CHRIS steps away.)* I think we should be friends, not enemies. So let's stop this silly nonsense about pollution, all right?

INQUISITOR.
> **THE CHURCH IS YOUR FRIEND**
> **YOU'RE IN OUR CONTROL**
> **THIS TORMENT MUST END**
> **WE'RE HERE FOR YOUR SOUL**
> **YOU SAY YOU HEAR VOICES**

JEANNE. Yes.

INQUISITOR.
> **FROM THE DEVIL**

JEANNE. No!

JACK. All that nonsense about the manure is a—projection, honey. You want to stir up some trouble because you're all mixed up about your mom selling your house and your brother being dead. But none of it's real. Can you see how your mind is playing tricks on you?

JEANNE.
> **I KNOW THAT MY VOICES ARE TRUE**
> **I'VE SEEN EVERYTHING THAT THEY'VE SAID**
> **MY GOD WOULD NOT LEAD ME—**

INQUISITOR.
YOUR GOD IS A DARKNESS
THAT SPEAKS WITH THE VOICE OF THE DEAD

JEANNE. No!

INQUISITOR.
YOU DRESS LIKE A MAN

JEANNE. Yes.

JACK.
YOUR MOTHER'S IN DEBT

CATHY. Wait—what?

INQUISITOR.
YOU SLEEP IN THE FIELDS

JEANNE. Yes.

JACK.
AND YOU'RE ALL UPSET

CATHY. Yeah, but—

INQUISITOR.
HEAR VOICES OF DEMONS

JEANNE. Y—no! My voices do not come from the devil!

JACK.
YOU'RE HAVING SUCH TROUBLE AT HOME

> **YOU'RE HAVING SUCH TROUBLE IN SCHOOL**
> **YOU'RE ONLY A KID—**

INQUISITOR.
> **YOU CAN'T READ OR WRITE**
> **WHAT—DO YOU TAKE US FOR FOOLS?**

CATHY.	JEANNE.
THIS IS NOT HAPPENING	**WHERE IS MY FAITH?**
BUT MAYBE IT IS	
MAYBE GOING CRAZY JUST FEELS	
LIKE THIS	
A GIRL OUT OF HISTORY	
AND MICHAEL WHO'S DEAD	
HOW CAN THIS NOT BE	
JUST IN MY HEAD?	

JEANNE.
> **CATHERINE, HELP ME!**

INQUISITOR.
> **YOU MUST BE A WITCH**
> **FOR ONLY A WITCH**
> **WOULD PRESUME TO HEAR GOD FROM THE**
>   **AIR**
> **REPENT FOR YOUR PRIDE**
> **ADMIT ALL YOUR LIES**
> **ACKNOWLEDGE YOUR SIN**
> **AND THE DANGER YOU'RE IN**
> **OR SAY YOUR LAST PRAYER**
> **AND BURN AT THE STAKE IF YOU DARE**

CATHY. Jeanne gets killed. *(She looks in JEANNE's eyes as the lights fade on her.)*

JACK. Cathy, what the sam hill— *(She gets up and looks in her book to make sure as JACK talks.)* This is nothing to get so upset about…

CHRIS. What's she doing now?

CATHY. She's dead. They kill her.

JACK. Shush, Chris. Cathy, is this about your brother?

CHRIS. She's crazy, I told you.

JACK. It's plain you're very confused. Listen, the factory expansion isn't gonna hurt a single thing.

CATHY. You're sure?

JACK. Expanding the factory is going to bring nothing but more jobs and more money—and that's all we need. Right, Chris? *(CHRIS nods.)* Cathy, I think I'll say a few words to your mother and then Chris and I will leave—

CHRIS. What about the report?

JACK. Chris. *(He exits to the house as CHRIS gives her an evil look.)*

CATHY. I was telling the truth. If the groundwater gets poisoned—

CHRIS. Blah, blah, blah. Fish. Trees. What's that to people having money and cars and homes and jobs? Wake up and live in the real world.

CATHY. Chris, why's he running for mayor? If all this town needs is more jobs… He could just buy our land, expand the factory and be done with it, couldn't he?

CHRIS. Uncle Jack wants to help people. It's called civic service.

CATHY. But I still don't see that that—

CHRIS. Keep your trap shut about that tree-hugging crap. You're just stirring up trouble.

(MIKE enters as CHRIS stomps off.)

MIKE. Cathy—

CATHY. You didn't tell me Jeanne was going to die. She did everything right and then they just— It's so unfair.

MIKE. You can't let that stop you from—

CATHY. Yes I can. Jack was right. I am worried about Mama selling this place and I am all messed up about you—being—you being dead—

MIKE. Cathy, that's exactly why I want—

CATHY. You say I should listen to you—but you're not even real, Mike. Jobs are real. Money is real. Mama is real. You're just a…I don't know what you are, but I want you to go away. I won't do this anymore. I'm scared—I'm scared I'm going crazy—

MIKE. What about Jeanne?

CATHY. She's dead. Like you.

(As MYRNA enters.)

MYRNA. Hey, honey…

CATHY. Oh, Mama.

(MUSIC #14: MYRNA COMFORTS CATHY - instrumental.)

MYRNA. Jack told me you had some kind of—

CATHY. …I was worried about the creek, and I…

MYRNA *(stroking her hair or patting her arm, reaching out)*. Honey. You really have to let this thing go.

MIKE. Cathy, please don't let it go.

CATHY. Mama. If you look at the articles I read—

MYRNA. Oh, I know what those articles say. The people who write them want farms to be like they were when I was a girl, but, Cathy... You can't really make a living farming anymore, unless you farm the way Jack does. I'll miss this house too and the creek, but— This place is gonna be a farm again. And that's...good. Can you see that?

MIKE. It's not just the creek you have to save.

MYRNA. I need you to be with me on this. Don't fight it anymore.

CATHY. Did I make you mess up signing those papers... with Jack?

MYRNA. No, you just delayed it a little. We'll get them signed after Jack's big rally, next week. You should come to that with me, Cathy. We've got to both start pulling for Jack's election. All right? Honey, I am sorry about your creek. If it could be any other way... *(Pause in MUSIC during following dialogue.)*

CATHY. I don't need the creek, Mama. It's just a sad place, like you said. And I should let it go. *(MYRNA leads her inside.)*

MIKE. Oh, Cathy. *(End MUSIC pause.)*

(Lights out on MIKE. Lights up on JASON, giving his report, CATHY coming in a little late.)

JASON. I decided to do my report on Galileo, who was a great scientist. He lived at a time when people believed that the sun and planets and stars and everything revolved around the earth. That's what it looks like, if you just look up. It looks like everything in the sky's circling around us. Anyway, Galileo took this new invention called the telescope, and looked up at the stars, and all of a sudden he could see stuff that people had never seen before. He started writing down what he saw in the sky. And some of the things he wrote and observed just…didn't fit with what people believed back then. He saw planets with moons revolving around them—like Jupiter? But how could that be if the Earth was the Center of the Universe? Right? Anyway, once people found out what Galileo was saying, they put him in prison—

CATHY. Why?

JASON. Well, because he was saying stuff that was pretty radical.

CATHY. So what? Can't a guy just say something?

MRS. MARSH. Cathy—hush! Jason is talking.

JASON. What Galileo had to say shook up everything that people thought was right and true and…no one wanted to change what they were thinking. No one wanted to change their view of the world. In fact, they'd rather kill Galileo than stop believing they were in the center of things, and more important than everything else in the sky.

CATHY. Did Galileo die in jail?

MRS. MARSH. Cathy—

JASON. Well, his jailers—priests mostly—said, "If you just admit you were wrong, we'll set you free."

CATHY. What did he do?

MRS. MARSH. This is very—

JASON. He lied. He said he was wrong. Otherwise they would have killed him.

CATHY. I thought you liked it when people told the truth.

JASON. I do. Except…

MRS. MARSH. Cathy, what in the world is going on? This is Jason's turn to speak. You're giving your report later this week.

CATHY. Yeah? I can give it to you right now. Joan of Arc saved half of France from the English soldiers and then she was captured and killed by her enemies. And no one tried to save her. They just let her burn. *(MUSIC #15: CATHY FRAGMENT. She leaves the classroom.)*
MRS. MARSH. Cathy, where do you think you're going?
CHRIS. She's such a fruitcake.

CATHY.	JASON.
NOW I KNOW THE TRUTH ABOUT	Shut up!
MY LIFE	
IN ORDER TO SURVIVE YOU	
HAVE TO LIE	
I'M DOING WHAT THEY WANT	CHRIS.
I ONLY HOPE IT'S WORTH THIS	She your girlfriend,
SAD GOODBYE...	Pritchard?

MRS. MARSH. Shush! Everyone! Is your report done, Jason?
JASON. I guess…I've said everything I need to say.

(Lights out on class. CATHY is at the creek.)

JASON *(off)*. Cathy!
CATHY *(as he enters)*. I'm sorry if I blew your report.
JASON. I don't care about that stupid report. *(He holds out a sheaf of papers.)* Listen. I found this on the Internet. It's a lot of stuff about factory farms and water.
CATHY. That project's done.
JASON. No, see, here's an article about a bunch of people in this town in Virginia, who lived right next to a factory farm, just like we do, all right?
CATHY. I don't care.

JASON. They all got sick, Cathy. Okay? Kids, mostly, but grownups too. The factory farm got so big, it couldn't contain the sewage...and the sewage overflowed and leaked, just like here, and it—it poisoned the groundwater and everyone in this town got all sorts of stuff wrong with them—babies born dead...and people with weird... cancers.

CATHY *(as MIKE enters)*. Like—like...?

JASON. Like your brother. Like my dad. Cathy, we have to get someone out here to test the water. And we have to stop DeCastro from expanding the factory until that happens—

CATHY. But the factory has to expand—

JASON. It might be killing us! Listen, there's ways to make sure the water around factories like his stay clean—but right now he doesn't have to make any improvements—

CATHY. I know, because the standards are ten years out of date—

JASON. And they'll stay that way as long as people like him are running the government. You get it?

CATHY. But, Jack's becoming mayor to help people—

JASON. Bull. He wants to be mayor so he can see to it the clean water regulations never change. I'd bet money on it, Cathy. Why else would he be spending all this time—

CATHY. We're just kids, Jason, no one's going to listen to us—

JASON. Yes, but the person who can really help us is your mom—

CATHY. My mom!

JASON. She's already working in the mayor's office. She's got a college degree. See, someone smart and important

has to call or write the Environmental Protection
Agency—
CATHY. My mom—
JASON. They will send someone, and then they can make
Jack DeCastro change how he does things, before more
people—
CATHY. My mom is going partners with Jack DeCastro,
okay?
JASON. You can make her listen! You can tell her—
CATHY. He's going to expand the factory on our land.
Right here! She's thrilled to death. *(Pause.)* Look, the
grownups have an answer for everything. They got
something to say about everything, and it's never what
you think is right. But they have to be right, Jason. They
have to be. Because—
JASON. Because?
CATHY. Because if they aren't…what does that say about
who's taking care of us? What does that say?
JASON. You know what's right, Cathy!
CATHY. So did Galileo! So did Joan of Arc! Look where
it got them!
JASON. You can really do something, here—
CATHY. No, I can't! Everyone should die. They're all stu-
pid anyway.
JASON. My dad should die? Your brother should die?
CATHY. Go away, Jason. Just go away. *(After a moment
he stomps off. Pause. MIKE enters.)* I don't want you to
be dead. I miss you, Michael.
MIKE. Cathy, you have to tell people.
CATHY. Mama will hate me. Jack will say I'm crazy. I
don't care if I get sick.
MIKE. It's not about getting sick.

CATHY. I don't want to live in a world where people get thrown in jail and burned alive for telling the truth.
MIKE. It's not about jail. It's about you.
CATHY. I'm not anybody, Mike.
MIKE. You're my star, okay? You're my little star.
CATHY. Mike, you're not even here!!
MIKE. Yes, I am. I am right here, Cathy.

(MUSIC #16: WHEN YOU KNOW THE TRUTH)

> **LISTEN, YOU HAVE GOT TO REALIZE**
> **PLEASE, YOU'VE GOT TO OPEN UP YOUR EYES**
> **THERE'S SOMEONE OVER THERE**
> **WHO DOESN'T EVEN CARE WHO LIVES OR**
>   **DIES**
>
> **I GET IT NOW, NOW IT'S REALLY CLEAR**
> **CATHY, THIS MUST BE WHY I AM HERE**
> **SO YOU COULD KNOW THE TRUTH**
> **AND RAISE YOUR VOICE TO SAVE WHAT YOU**
>   **HOLD DEAR**

(CATHY shakes her head, he grabs her.)

> **WHEN YOU KNOW THE TRUTH, IT HAS A**
>   **NAME.**
> **AND WHEN YOU KNOW ITS NAME, IT KNOWS**
>   **YOURS TOO.**
> **NOW YOU KNOW THE TRUTH**
> **AND NOW YOU KNOW WHAT YOU MUST DO.**
>
> **THIS ISN'T JUST THE CREEK, OR YOU, OR ME.**
> **IT'S BIGGER, NOW, BY FAR, THAN WE CAN SEE.**
> **IF YOU LOOK THE OTHER WAY, AND WASTE**
>   **ANOTHER DAY**
> **OR TWO OR THREE.**

YOU'LL NEVER KNOW THE ANSWER
TO HOW MUCH YOU COULD HAVE SAVED
YOU'LL NEVER KNOW
YOU HAVE NO WAY OF KNOWING
IF YOU TURN YOUR BACK ON EVERYTHING
   ALIVE
AND KID YOURSELF, THINKING YOU SURVIVED
WHEN THE TRUTH YOU WOULDN'T SAY
KEEPS POUNDING EVERY DAY
DOWN DEEP INSIDE

WHEN YOU KNOW THE TRUTH, IT HAS A
   NAME.
AND WHEN YOU KNOW ITS NAME, IT KNOWS
   YOURS TOO.
NOW YOU KNOW THE TRUTH
AND NOW YOU KNOW WHAT YOU MUST DO.

CATHY. Mike, if I do this, I'll just wind up like Jeanne.

(Lights up on JEANNE. Her trial is over.)

JEANNE *(does not know CATHY is there)*. Oh, Lady
   Catherine. Have all my voices forsaken me?
CATHY. Jeanne, I…
JEANNE. Oh, please say it is not some trick of my mind!
   Catherine, please say you are truly there.
CATHY. I'm here. I'm here, Jeanne.
MYRNA *(off)*. Cathy! It's time to go to Jack's rally. He
   wants us both there, hon.
CATHY. I can't stay long.

JEANNE. They say I am to die, Lady Catherine. They say I am a witch and all the English army waits outside to see me burn. Catherine, I have failed in my task!

CATHY. No, Jeanne…

JEANNE. My king has forsaken me, France is lost and Catherine—I lied!

CATHY. You?

JEANNE. There were no voices for so long. Only the priests, asking me the same questions, over and over. I felt so alone. Then one morning, my captors took me outside and they showed me a great pile of wood. Oh, Catherine, as big as a house, this stack, all fresh laid. And they said, "This is what we have made for you. And this is where you will burn tomorrow unless you swear to us now that your voices are lies!" And, Catherine, I betrayed you. I said, "Yes, I will say whatever you want! Only do not burn me! I am afraid to die!"

CATHY. You were scared, that's all…

JEANNE. I was weak. The next morning I tore up the paper they made me sign, so they will kill me now. But it is too late, is it not? I have lied, and I have failed and France is no more.

(MUSIC #17: JEANNE/CATHY FRAGMENT)

**I HAVE DONE WHAT I SHOULD NOT HAVE DONE
I HAVE HID AND HAVE FAILED AND HAVE RUN
NOW I SIT IN MY CELL OF STONE
AND I'M SCARED AND I'M SO ALONE**

CATHY. No, no. Listen.

ONE GIRL CAN CHANGE THE WORLD

You didn't fail, Jeanne. France is totally still around, I promise. Five hundred years later. They must have slammed the English good.

JEANNE. Oh, Catherine, you bring me such relief. I have been so frightened.

CATHY. I'm sorry. I got scared too. But it's better now with you here.

JEANNE. I have so longed for my home these last weeks. I have thought—if only I did not do this thing God asked—I could be home with my mother, on the farm. In April I thought of the little lambs being born. Lady, they are so dear and small and warm. I shall never see them again…

CATHY. But you couldn't lie to those stupid English priests and then just go back home…

JEANNE. No, I could not…

CATHY. If you'd said everything you believed in was a lie… If you'd lied and just gone home…you would be alive—but you'd be—

MYRNA *(off)*. Cathy! Shake a leg, here!

CATHY *(looking off where her mother's voice came from)*. You'd be someone else. You'd be lost. *(Beat.)* I have to go, Jeanne. I have to do something. *(She takes MIKE's hand.)*

JEANNE. Catherine, be brave.

CATHY. I'll think about you, and that will make me brave.

(MUSIC #18: THE RALLY)

(The rally forms around JACK as he enters on the song. CATHY, MYRNA, MICHAEL, JEANNE, all there along with the rest of the CAST.)

JACK.
> **LONG TIME AGO, WAY BEFORE TV**
> **THINGS WERE DIFFERENT THEN, BELIEVE YOU ME.**
> **YOU HAD YOUR LITTLE FARM,**
> **AND EVEN THOUGH IT WASN'T EASY,**
> **IT WAS SIMPLE, IF YOU KNOW WHAT I MEAN.**
> **BUT THE WORLD IS BIGGER**
> **AND WE'VE GOTTA KEEP UP TO MAKE SURE**
> **IT DOESN'T LEAVE US BEHIND**
> **YOU'RE LOOKING AT THE MAN**
> **WITH A VISIONARY PLAN**
> **THE BEST THAT YOU'RE GONNA FIND**
> **VOTE FOR ME, YOU'LL SEE**
> **MONEY SO WE ALL SUCCEED**
> **SIMPLE AS YOUR ABC'S**
> **DECASTRO'S THE ONE YOU NEED**

(As the CROWD cheers.) I promise you a Trawling where everyone has a good job and a hot meal at the end of the day! Look how far Trawling has already come through my efforts. And you know I did it for you! For the town I love. I grew up in this place, on a little farm. Some of you might remember what the DeCastro Farms used to look like—

CATHY. Mama, you have to listen to me.

MYRNA. What is this, Cathy? *(As CATHY hands her the papers JASON delivered.)*

JACK. Little red barn, little red wagon. *(NOTE: The sometimes lengthy pauses between JACK's lines can be filled with handshakes and sotto voce additions and ad libs. CATHY and MYRNA continue to argue silently during their pauses.)*

CATHY. We have to tell Jack not to expand the factory. It's really important.

JACK. That's what a farm was in the old days. That's all it needed to be. But times change and Trawling's got to change along with the times.

MYRNA. Cathy, not now…

JACK. It's a new time for us all. Can you feel it?

CATHY. Mike might have gotten sick from the factory, like those people in those pages.

MYRNA. Honey, I'm sure Jack knows best. Really, he wouldn't—

JACK. And comes a time when you need a little more than a little red barn and a little red wagon.

CATHY. I'm sorry this is going to hurt you. *(She starts toward JACK's platform.)*

JACK. You need more than just a little plot of land and little dream.

MYRNA *(crumpling the papers)*. Cathy, come back here!

JEANNE.
    I AM ONLY ONE GIRL…

JACK. It's a bigger world than it used to be.

MYRNA. Honey, you don't even know for sure if this is true—

JEANNE.
    I AM ONLY ONE
    I CAN ONLY DO SO MUCH…

JACK. There's a big picture! Let me hear you, people! Can you see the big picture!

ENSEMBLE. Yes!

MYRNA. There's no proof— *(Grabbing her.)*

JACK. And furthermore—I'll change the way we think in Trawling, Iowa!

JEANNE.
> **I AM ONLY ONE GIRL**

CATHY. It's Mike I'm thinking of, Mama—

JEANNE.
> **WITH MY ONLY ONE VOICE THAT CAN ONLY UNDO SO MUCH**
> **THERE'S SO MUCH TO UNDO**

MYRNA. Cathy—this is our future, here.

JACK. Let's think about prosperity! Let's think about courage!

MYRNA. This is just your fear talking.

JEANNE.
> **BUT ONE GIRL CAN CHANGE THE WORLD**
> **YES, ONE GIRL CAN CHANGE THE WORLD**

CATHY. No, Mama. You're the one who's afraid. You're the one who's not seeing what's right here.

JACK. Let's talk about vision!

CATHY *(pulls away from her, yelling)*. Excuse me, Mr. DeCastro—!

JEANNE.	JACK.
WE MAY THINK WE'RE ALONE WE MAY THINK WE HAVE ONLY OUR ONE SMALL LIFE TO LIVE	But it's like this, folks. If you buy into a piece of the big picture there's always something in it for you.

CATHY. Jack!
JACK. Not now, Cathy.

JEANNE.	JACK.
BUT THIS IS BIGGER THAN US WE'VE GOT TO STAY WIDE AWAKE, THERE ARE MANY MORE LIVES AT STAKE AND BRAVE STEPS YET TO TAKE	You just have to ask the right questions, and then you start hearing the right answers and I have the answer right here in my hand, a loan application for three million—

CATHY. I have a question!
JACK. Not now.
JASON. Let her ask!
CATHY *(in sudden silence)*. What about the water in Trawling, Iowa, Mr. DeCastro? What are you going to do about that?
JASON. Cathy! Yes, the water!
CATHY. An expansion of your factory can really—I think—I think maybe the groundwater in Trawling, Iowa, has been—messed up—
JASON. Fatally contaminated—
CATHY. Yeah! Fatally contaminated!
JASON. With carcinogens!
CATHY. By your factories! And I think—I can prove it!
JACK. Cathy. You don't know what you're talking about…
JASON. Well, I do! I know all about it!
JACK. Myrna, will you tell—

CATHY. My brother might have died from the runoff you've been hosing into the ground—you're using—outdated technology—and faulty—waste removal—processes—

JASON. Go, Cathy!

CATHY. And if you expand the factory, it won't make things better, it will make things worse, much worse.

JASON. My dad's sick—Sam Macafee's sick—Josie Callahan's sick—we could all get sick—

JACK. Myrna, do something with your fool child, for heaven's sake, she's babbling—

CATHY. What would happen if we tested the water?

JACK. I already told you, my factory is in complete compliance—

CATHY. I didn't ask if your factory was in compliance! I want to know what would happen if we tested the water here in this town, right now?

JACK. I don't have to answer these questions, right now. Myrna, will you—

CATHY. Mama, please see this.

MYRNA. Jack, there's only one way to know for sure.

JACK. This—this is a little girl talking!

MYRNA. If there's the slightest chance what Cathy's saying is true…

JACK. She talks to herself! She's deluded—

MYRNA. I'm not signing away my farm until I know—

JACK. Now listen here— Don't think you can take me on because I got backers—

MYRNA. Well, I have a son who's dead. And a daughter who says that might have something to do with you. Are you going to stand up in front of the whole town right

here and tell me that doesn't bear some investigation? *(Crowd murmurs.)*
JACK. This town is nothing without DeCastro Farms, Myrna, and you are nothing without my holdings—
MYRNA. How dare you?

(MUSIC #19: FINALE)

THERE IS MORE TO THIS TOWN
MORE CONNECTION, MORE KNOW-HOW
THAN WE CAN IMAGINE HERE

JACK.
BUT YOU'RE ALL GOIN' DOWN

MYRNA. No, we're not!
WE'RE GONNA STAND UP AND HOLD IT
** TOGETHER**
THIS MUCH IS CLEAR
THIS MUCH IS CRYSTAL CLEAR

MYRNA & JEANNE.
NOW WE ALL CAN SAVE THIS LAND
NOW WE ALL CAN
TAKE TOMORROW BY THE HAND
UNDERSTAND
WHAT IT TAKES TO COME INTO YOUR OWN
** COMMAND**
TO TAKE A STAND

CATHY. You see her!
MYRNA. Cathy. I see you, I see you, honey.
JACK. Myrna, honestly, if you would just see—

MYRNA. Oh, Jack. I'm seeing things just fine.
  **MY DAUGHTER KNEW THE TRUTH, SHE HAD
    THE GUTS
  TO STAND UP TO SOMEONE LIKE YOU
  WHAT AM I, NUTS!?
  IT WAS ALL THERE, I KNEW THE SCORE
  BUT I WAS TIRED OF BEING POOR
  AND YOU KNEW THAT
  YOU DIRTY RAT
  BUT NOW I'M WIDE AWAKE, I'M READY FOR
  A GUST OF WIND, A BRAND NEW DAY
  AN OPEN DOOR, AN OPEN DOOR...**
(MIKE's hand rests on her shoulder, and she can feel it.)
Go on, Jack. Go on and tell us all here that you care more about your cash flow than you do about our lives.
JACK. Well, I wouldn't say that, of course...
CATHY. So Mama can call someone to test the water?
MYRNA. Yes. We'll be testing the water several times, I think, before we build anything on my farm. Jack. *(He exits, disgusted.)*
  **FROM FAR AWAY
  IT SEEMS SO SIMPLE
  THIS TOWN IS JUST A TINY PLACE**

JASON & CATHY & MYRNA.
  **FROM FAR AWAY
  WE'RE ALL THE SAME
  EVERYBODY KEEPIN' UP THE PACE**

MYRNA, JEANNE, MIKE, JASON, CATHY.
  **BUT LOOK UP CLOSE
  THE WATER FLOWS
  IT'S FLOWING THROUGH OUR DAYS AND
    NIGHTS**

ALL.
> **AND IF WE PAY ATTENTION NOW**
> **WE'RE GONNA WAKE UP AND REALIZE**
> **YOU GOTTA STOP AND LOOK UP CLOSE**
> **OR YOU'LL MISS THE STUFF YOU WANNA SEE**
> **THE MOST**
> **IF YOU START WITH ONE HEART**
> **AND THE COURAGE TO STICK**
> **EVEN WHEN THE WHOLE WORLD SAYS NO**
> **THE POWER OF THAT ONE HEART**
> **GIVES ITS COURAGE AND LOVE**
> **TO THE REST OF THE WHOLE WIDE WORLD**
> **AND EVERYONE IS CHANGED**
> **NOW WE ALL CAN CHANGE OUR WORLD**

(During the song, there is an opportunity for everyone to connect with CATHY. Not everyone would probably give her a big hug, but certainly CHRIS might pat her back and ADELAIDE might concede a handshake. The stage empties gradually. MYRNA is the last to leave and hug CATHY. MIKE takes JEANNE's hand. By the end of the song all have exited except CATHY, MIKE, JEANNE and JASON.)

CATHY.
> **AND ONE GIRL CAN CHANGE THE WORLD**
For you the moon, Mike. *(MIKE nods. He holds CATHY's look and then exits with JEANNE.)*

JASON. I'm glad you told the truth.

CATHY. Oh, well. Thanks for being there, and being so smart.

JASON. Thanks for being braver than Galileo.

CATHY. Hey, Jason…I…there's this dance girls are supposed to ask boys to go to…
JASON. Uh-huh?
CATHY. Will you go with me?
JASON. Yeah. I'd like that.
CATHY. Cool. There's a problem, though.
JASON. What?
CATHY. I can't dance.
JASON. That's easy. You just…like hold each other.
CATHY. Uh-huh…
JASON. And you move around in a circle. More or less.
CATHY. Like a binary system?
JASON. Yeah.
CATHY. Think that's what we look like to everything up there? *(She points at the sky.)*
JASON. I don't know.
CATHY. Well. I'm gonna say we do.

(The lights fade out, and we see them standing together under the stars, looking up.)

END OF PLAY

DIRECTOR'S NOTES

DIRECTOR'S NOTES

DIRECTOR'S NOTES